THE UNOFFICIAL BTS BIBLE

ALL OF THE FACTS YOU NEED ON K-POP'S BIGGEST SENSATIONS!

DIANNE PINEDA-KIM

Racehorse Publishing

Copyright © 2020 by Dianne Pineda-Kim

Photographs copyright © 2020 by gettyimages unless otherwise noted

All rights reserved. No part of this book may be reproduced in any manner without the express written consent of the publisher, except in the case of brief excerpts in critical reviews or articles. All inquiries should be addressed to Racehorse Publishing, 307 West 36th Street, 11th Floor, New York, NY 10018.

Racehorse Publishing books may be purchased in bulk at special discounts for sales promotion, corporate gifts, fund-raising, or educational purposes. Special editions can also be created to specifications. For details, contact the Special Sales Department, Skyhorse Publishing, 307 West 36th Street, 11th Floor, New York, NY 10018 or info@skyhorsepublishing.com.

Racehorse Publishing™ is a pending trademark of Skyhorse Publishing, Inc.®, a Delaware corporation.

Visit our website at www.skyhorsepublishing.com.

10 9 8 7 6 5 4 3 2 1

Library of Congress Cataloging-in-Publication Data is available on file.

Cover design by Brian Peterson
Cover photography by Getty Images
Interior photography by Getty Images

ISBN: 978-1-63158-597-5
E-Book ISBN: 978-1-63158-598-2

Printed in China

Table of Contents

CHAPTER 1

BOYS WITH BIG DREAMS

BTS performing "Fake Love" at the 2018 Billboard Music Awards in Las Vegas, Nevada.

"IT DOESN'T MAKE SENSE THAT WE'RE HERE," Jimin, one of the members of BTS, said in Korean as he looked around wide-eyed at the MGM Grand Garden Arena in Las Vegas, where the 2018 Billboard Music Awards (BBMAs) were being held. Its halls were reverberating with the name of their group as more than half of the 17,000-seat venue was filled with their fans cheering for them.

The rest of his bandmates were in utter disbelief, too. "It's fascinating, it's still fascinating," RM repeated to himself. "Famous people coming to us to say hi," Jin quipped, trying to keep his emotions in check.

A mixture of trepidation, excitement, and wonder could be seen on their faces. It was

their defining moment, one among many that have signaled that these seven twenty-something South Korean men have arrived on the world stage.

Everything was a blur, like a daydream flashing right before their eyes. Even before they sat in the front row in what was considered one of music's biggest nights, they exchanged pleasantries with music personalities they could only imagine meeting in real life. American DJ and record executive DJ Khaled talked to the boys as though they were old friends. Taylor Swift, whose chart-topping hits and personal life gets extensive media coverage, knocked on their dressing room door and asked if they could all take a photo together. "She's even taller with heels!" one of the members exclaimed before they were all whisked away to meet yet another revered artist: John Legend. V has been a fan of the singer-songwriter for over ten years and was the first to hug John, who, in turn, greeted them with a loud *"Annyeonghaseyo!"* J-Hope wanted to make sure they had their photo taken together with his phone, and much to their surprise, John pulled out a copy of their album *Love Yourself: Tear* and asked them to sign it because his daughter is a big fan. "You guys are blowing up in America, that's huge! But you guys are already big everywhere else," John said. Suga and Jungkook then shyly looked at

each other as one said, "I still can't believe John Legend pulled out our album from his own bag!"

A little later they found rapper and producer Pharrell Williams waiting for them backstage, telling them, "We gotta work together now! Let's set it up!" It was another starstruck moment for Jin, who with his mouth agape after the encounter, said jokingly, "I was going in for a hand kiss, but I restrained myself."

All the big names in the music industry wanted to collaborate with them. All the cameras flashed in their direction and everyone wanted to get a glimpse of the band who took the world by storm.

BTS enjoying the BBMAs on the front row alongside top music celebrities.

In a matter of minutes, BTS would be performing for the first time at the 2018 BBMAs, after big acts like Ariana Grande, Ed Sheeran, Jennifer Lopez, Khalid, Christina Aguilera, among many others—and it was on that same stage where acclaimed pop icon Janet Jackson sang a medley of her iconic hits as the recipient of the Billboard Music Icon Award.

"Let's welcome the biggest boy band in the world!" Kelly Clarkson, a Billboard Chart record-breaker herself, introduced BTS before the band delivered their impeccably choreographed song, "Fake Love."

As the spotlight turned to them on a stage that was considerably smaller than the ones they had trodden before, their haunting music, palpable energy, slick moves, and Korean lyrics filled the venue. The audience's screams almost overpowered the group's sound, with everyone trying to sing familiar lines and calling out the members' names with their official fan chant: "Kim Nam Joon! Kim Seok-jin! Min Yoon-gi! Jung Ho-seok! Park Jimin! Kim Taehyung! Jeon Jungkook! B-T-S! B-T-S!"

It was a sight that not many in the US had ever seen before: a largely diverse audience singing and dancing to a non-English song and truly having the time of their lives. At that moment, these young men's charisma and talents became bigger than that stage.

"I was so nervous I felt like I could die!" Jimin said as he left the stage.

BTS backstage at the 2018 BBMAs.

The septet has been experiencing a lot of big things for the first time since they set foot in the US aside from the BBMAs: the explosive debut of their song "DNA" at the American Music Awards in 2017, appearances on some of the most recognizable TV talk shows, and concert tours in different states.

Each of the members always seems like he's unaffected by the group's not-so-newfound fame: being genuinely amazed as they first boarded their tour bus ("We've only seen this in documentaries of foreign artists!" one of the boys exclaimed), goofing around backstage, and unglamorously munching on hot dogs before their guest appearance on *The Ellen DeGeneres Show.*

"We're just a normal group of boys from humble backgrounds who had a lot of passion and dreams," RM said in an interview with *Time* magazine.[1] This relatability and accessibility seem to resonate with fans no matter what age, nationality, gender, or background.

"They are real. They show that their lives are not much different from ours. They are the same as us. Otherwise they would never gain this level of popularity," Yun Jeung Jo, Executive Director of Korean Cultural Center New York, said in an interview with CNBC.[2]

"It's like you grow up with them, I feel like they're my family and my friends," one of the BTS fans said during a concert in Seoul.[3]

BTS wins Top Social Artist at the 2018 BBMAs.

Rubbing elbows with top stars and touring to sold-out shows in the US are by no means their only measure of success. BTS's incredible trajectory to stardom was made up of several factors: their inspiring music; candid, honest personalities; unique promotion strategy; and one-of-a-kind connection with fans. This book is only a peek at how they were able to grow their fanbase to record-breaking levels. Their narrative is much more layered than a story of small-town boys who achieved their dreams of being stars.

But what does it really mean to "make it" in this billion-dollar music industry? Is it the record sales and chart-topping hits? The brand endorsements? The legions of fans? Living the life of famous pop stars?

This book aims to explore how BTS stretched the boundaries of K-pop and went beyond the stereotypes, the story of their highs and lows, the overarching message of their music, and ultimately, how they enforced the fundamental idea that making it means being true to yourself. That night at the BBMAs, and all the other prestigious award shows they have participated in, are far from being the culmination of their careers. Rather, it's only the beginning.

BTS stole the attention on the 2018 BBMAs red carpet with their unique styles.

CHAPTER 2

BTS BY THE NUMBERS

"TODAY WE ARE MAKING HISTORY," RM SAYS AS he leads the group's practice of joining their hands together to say a little prayer or motivational words right before every performance. He couldn't have been any more right. In the short span since their debut, BTS's career has reached milestone after milestone, and has been featured in headline after headline.

BTS, which is composed of members RM, Jin, Suga, J-Hope, Jimin, V, and Jungkook, is an acronym for "*Bangtan Sonyeondan*" in Korean, which literally translates to "Bulletproof Boy Scouts" in English. In 2017 their company, Big Hit Entertainment, added the acronym "Beyond the Scene" to their name, perhaps to make it more universal and connect more with their international fans. The company explained their new brand identity as: "BTS protecting the youths from prejudice. They are moving forward, chasing their dreams, instead of settling for reality."[4]

Moving forward they did, overtaking contemporary artists and setting new standards along the way. It's hard to talk about BTS without mentioning the numbers and records they have broken during their rapid rise to superstardom. While numbers and superlatives often run short of encapsulating their long and hard-fought journey, it is these details that make up the whole of their story.

BTS members always show their fun personalities on the red carpet.

"K-pop band BTS have done it again," Guinness World Records declares as it announces yet another feat from the band. They have sold millions of albums just in their homeland of South Korea, but their ascent around the world keeps on going. As the records continue to grow in popularity, Aja Romano of the Vox news site surmised that the band "would go on to completely transform the image of all-male boy bands in South Korean music and shatter conceptions of what breakout success looked like for South Korean bands overseas."[5]

They have reached many "first Korean Artist" achievements, particularly on the Billboard Charts, which are a credible key measure of album success in the US for any artist, as Billboard collects data and "publishes a host of charts that are individually or collectively based on key fan interactions with music, including album sales and downloads, track downloads, radio airplay and touring as well as streaming and social interactions on Facebook, Twitter, Vevo, YouTube, Spotify, and other popular online destinations for music."[6]

These achievements include being the first Korean artists to top the Billboard 200. Their

The USA and the rest of the world fell in love with BTS and their music touched the hearts of many.

album *Love Yourself: Tear* reached number one for a week in June 2018, a remarkable feat where Billboard also notes that this was "the first primarily foreign language No. 1 album in over 12 years" on the chart, since the music is performed mostly in Korean.[7] It is the highest ranking any Korean artist has ever achieved, the previous holder being BTS themselves when they placed at number seven. They did it again, as Guinness exclaimed, with their albums *Love Yourself: Answer* and *Map of the Soul: Persona* reaching top spots, making them the first-ever Korean artists with three albums on the Billboard 200 simultaneously. In comparison, the Beatles had a similar feat, sending three albums to the number one spot in the US in less than a year. "Before BTS, the last traditional group (excluding the Glee ensemble, whose multiple cast members rotated) to log three leaders within such a quick span was the Beatles in 1995-96, when the band's archival releases 'Anthology 1,' 'Anthology 2' and 'Anthology 3' all debuted at No. 1 in a stretch of 11 months and a week," Billboard said.[8]

In 2018, BTS achieved two Gold albums in the US, as the Recording Industry Association of America (RIAA) announced that *Love Yourself: Answer* made history as the first album by a Korean artist to receive a RIAA Gold certification. A year after, *Map of the Soul: Persona* received an official Gold

BTS wins their third consecutive Top Social Artist Award at the 2019 BBMAs, with RM stating: "This means so much for us, we'll do our best today."

certification after selling over half a million units.[9] In January 2020, *Love Yourself: Answer* surpassed one million sales and streams, making it the first album by a Korean artist to receive a RIAA Platinum certification.[10]

BTS has been making their presence known on the Billboard charts since 2015 (before what the media often refers to as their "US takeover"), when their album, *The Most Beautiful Moment in Life, Pt. 2* peaked at top 171.[11]

It is apparent that while their achievements in South Korea are an entirely different story, BTS has been capturing the attention of international audiences long before they reached number one in the US.

Their numbers are not only rising in the US and South Korea—their presence has also been noticed in major charts around the world. In the United Kingdom, another market that is considerably difficult to crack, BTS's *Wings* became the first Korean album to rank on the UK Official Albums Chart. They did it several other times with their consecutive albums, as Jack White wrote about the album *Map of the Soul: Persona*, "If the group keeps up their momentum, it will mark their highest charting release yet in the UK and become the first Number 1 album from a Korean act on the Official Chart."[12] The international preorders for the album back then were equally impressive:

RM, Jin, Suga, J-Hope, Jimin, V, and Jungkook of BTS perform on *Good Morning America* on May 15, 2019 in New York City.

the total number reached a whopping 3,021,822. Meanwhile, Big Hit announced that a month before the February 21, 2020 release of their latest album *Map of the Soul: 7*, the stock preorders reached 3.42 million recorded, surpassing preorders for *Map of the Soul: Persona* well before the end of the presale period.[13] As of the writing of this book, preorders for *Map of the Soul: 7* have reached 4.02 million copies, making it the most pre-ordered South Korean album of all time.[14] As of June 15, 2020, it was reported by Forbes that the album claimed "fifth most weeks on the sales ranking among Korean albums." It also landed No. 1 on the Billboard 200 chart, claiming one of the biggest releases in 2020.

According to a report by *Soompi*, their single "Black Swan," As of June 15, 2020, it was reported by Forbes that the album claimed "fifth most weeks on the sales ranking among Korean albums." It also landed No. 1 on the Billboard 200 chart, claiming one of the biggest releases in 2020. hit number one on iTunes Top Songs charts in at least 93 different regions—their highest number to date—including the United States, Canada, Mexico, the United Kingdom, France, Germany, Brazil, Argentina, Saudi Arabia, India, Russia, and more.[15]

Over at the Oricon Charts, the longest standing music and entertainment statistics and ranking provider in Japan, BTS garnered another record high when their Japanese single "MIC Drop/DNA/Crystal Snow" managed to hit number thirteen on Oricon's 2017 singles chart, the highest ranking ever achieved by a K-pop artist.[16] It is also important to note that the band has been constantly charting in Oricon due to their Japanese-language single promotions.

Back home in South Korea, the results also mirrored their successes abroad. *Love Yourself: Her* sold 1.6 million copies in South Korea, the most copies to ever sell in the history of the Gaon Music Chart.[17] Meanwhile, almost all of BTS's albums fly off the shelves within their first week of release, with two of them achieving one million sales each, setting a new record at the Hanteo Charts.[18] This is the highest number of albums recorded on Hanteo in the first week since release, ever since the chart's creation in 1993, at that time earning BTS the title in South Korea as "double million seller and all-chart killer."

Map of the Soul: Persona topped Nielsen Music's Top 10 Physical Albums chart for the first half of 2019 with sales of 312,000 copies in the US alone. In its section "K-Pop Global Domination," the Nielsen Music Mid-Year Report US 2019 credited BTS as one of the groups that led to the popularity of K-pop in the international scene: "After achieving record consumption in 2018, K-Pop reached a new critical mass this year, thanks to new releases from supergroup BTS and BLACKPINK."[19]

Their ever-growing fanbase and increasing record breaks opened more opportunities for them to stand on bigger stages: BTS presented the award for the Best R&B Album at the sixty-first Grammy Awards in February 2019, and made their *Saturday Night Live* debut in April 2019, another first as Korean artists.

BTS presents the award for Best R&B Album at the 61st Annual Grammy Awards at the Staples Center on February 10, 2019 in Los Angeles, California. "Growing up in South Korea, we always dreamed about being on the Grammy stage," RM said amidst thunderous applause.

BTS with multiple Grammy Award–winner Alicia Keys backstage.

"Growing up in South Korea, we always dreamed of being on the Grammys stage," RM addressed the crowd in English when BTS went onstage as presenters. "Thank you to all our fans for making this dream come true and we'll be back."

BTS kept that promise, returning to the Grammys stage in 2020 to perform "Old Town Road" with Lil Nas X and several other artists. This performance made BTS the first Korean group to perform at the Grammys.

The numbers indeed don't lie. But these are just an overview of their several other landslide sweeps. BTS likely will have broken more records by the time this book is published. And they're only just getting started.

BTS's agency's CEO, Bang Si-Hyuk,

however, emphasized in a lecture that he doesn't want the group to obsess on results and records. "Music is not the Olympics. We should focus on what kind of music we make and what messages to show," he said.

"While achievements are important, we hope to give our fans happiness above all else," RM said. "It's a real honor," J-Hope told *Time*, via a translator. "We're proud that everything we do is giving off light."[20]

In an analysis of BTS's victories and the reasons that led to them, Grammy.com notes, "It's become increasingly clear that the K-pop titans are currently the most visible representatives of where mainstream pop music—American pop music in particular—is headed."[21]

CHAPTER 3

THE POWER OF THE ARMYS

I hear your voice
Within the noise, time stops
We are connected by sound

When I close my eyes
In the darkness, your light
Lights the way for me
We can walk forward without fear, you and I

You're my light, you're my light
Always shine into my heart
You're my light, you're my light
No matter how far apart we are
Your light shines on me
— **BTS, "Lights"**[22]

FOR PEOPLE WHO MAY NOT BE FAMILIAR WITH
BTS, the quantifying facts and statistics may
prove helpful in getting to know them and
realizing the scope of their influence. For fans,
these numbers are a part of their shared
efforts and contributions, with each and every
vote, view, follow, album, or ticket sale adding
a stepping stone to their success.

Their fans are officially called ARMY, which
stands for "Adorable Representative M.C.
for Youth." The meaning is different from the
literal "army," a loyal legion that protects their
country. The BTS ARMY has an inextricable
bond with BTS, as represented by the band's
official logo—a bulletproof vest. If reversed, the
ARMY's logo forms a shield. This is meaningful
for both the fans and the band, where the
interchangeable roles of supporter, leader,
protector, and follower are mutually shared.

For Jimin, their fans are far from strangers.

"Regarding my life, my members and ARMY are
like heroes to me, although I'm the one who's
supposed to be everyone's hero," he explained
in an interview. "I've had hard times where I was
about to break, where I became depressed
and reached rock bottom. During those times,
the members and ARMY always stayed by my
side."[23] Jungkook shares the same sentiment:
"They're happy about the smallest things and
love what we do. And that gives us comfort too."

The ARMYs are not just like any other large
fanbase that past and present megastars
have had. In this digitally powered and highly
connected generation, worldwide BTS fans have
found a way to forge a close relationship with
the group, one that many music experts say has
yet to be achieved by any other artist.

"A seven-man hit factory with a mobilised,
Internet-driven fanbase known as the ARMY,
BTS occupy a powerful position in modern
pop, reflective of a progressive new era of
music that crosses borders, genres and
language, something all the more striking
considering the eagerness with which nations
are building walls," Adam White of the *Daily
Telegraph* mused.[24]

As of this writing, the band has over 26.5
million followers on their official Twitter (@
BTS_twt), 21.2 million followers on their second
account (@bts_bighit), 31.3 million subscribers
on YouTube (Bangtan TV), 26.2 million followers
on their Instagram (@bts.bighitofficial) and more
than 11.4 million followers on Facebook.

A photo of BTS member Jin getting out
of a car upon arrival at a red-carpet event

became a global Twitter trend as people referred to him as the "car door guy." A live video of two members applying face masks, doing a *"mukbang"* (eating while talking online), a photo of V's head-to-toe airport fashion, and a single selfie from Jimin sitting by the airplane window can easily acquire a million views. But in the wide and certainly anonymous digital expanse, how do people even begin to find their content?

The simple answer is that the members do not have their own individual accounts. They are given autonomy in uploading their whereabouts or thoughts through the umbrella of their official BTS accounts, enabling fans to congregate easily on shared sites. Unlike other K-pop groups whose members have varying followers on SNS, depending on what the fans call their "bias," BTS comes in one whole package. Once you like one of them, you like them all.

Communities start and grow when safe spaces are built for people to converse, exchange, and interact. Big Hit Entertainment is fully aware of this, which is why they launched an entirely new app called Weverse, made especially for BTS fans and other artists managed by the company. This is a reinvention of online fancafés or fansites, but instead of the typical blog posts, this innovation allows the band members to post real-time photos and updates, and "funny, touching, or inspirational" posts in the feature called Artist Moments, which expire after twenty-four hours. This is a game changer in the scene because, not only does it have a fan-friendly environment between BTS and ARMYs, it also has a built-in translator that accommodates non-

Korean-speaking fans. Without discontinuing traditional social media networks like Twitter, Facebook, Naver V Live, and Instagram, Weverse consolidates them all in one place. It is both exclusive and inclusive at the same time.

"It's a team effort taken from what happens to us in our everyday life. It's not easy to run a social media account over a long period of time, but we love communicating with our fans every day and night," RM told *Time*. "For example, I use the hashtag #RMusic to introduce or recommend a song I like, and I've been doing that for a long time. I love music and I truly enjoy sharing with our fans. Music transcends language. BTS communicates with our fans by staying true to ourselves and believing in music every day."

BTS is also a lesson in social media marketing that many brands and artists are now taking inspiration from. The big difference lies in the ARMYs' level and frequency of engagement. They are not, in any way, just bystanders or "lurkers" that simply scroll through the content that BTS churns out—they watch their videos, stream their music, reply to and share their posts. The fans make their support tangible and known to the band by collectively being responsive to each member of the band's efforts.

The ARMYs, no doubt, are active and interactive participants that continue to propel the band's fame to new heights. To put this in perspective, BTS garnered yet another Guinness Record for Most Twitter Engagement for a music group, with their account registering 422,228 engagements on Twitter as of April 29, 2019. Bufferapp.com describes a Twitter engagement as the "total number of times a user interacts with a Tweet. Clicks anywhere on the Tweet, including retweets, replies, follows, likes, links, cards, hashtags, embedded media, username, profile photo or Tweet expansion"[25] are counted. This means that BTS's fans don't just read about them on Twitter. They respond, share, discuss, and expand the Tweet, allowing it to reach millions of people around the globe.

"The BTS community is so nice, it's very lively, and the interaction between BTS and their fans on Twitter is insane," Phoebe, a fan interviewed by the *Telegraph* at a BTS concert in London, explained. "It's so diverse and the most accepting community I've ever been a part of, more than school."[26]

Additionally, the power of the ARMY is visible on the music streaming app Spotify, where BTS became the first K-pop group, and Asian artist overall, to surpass five billion streams on the platform. Their song "Fake Love" was Spotify's most-streamed K-pop track of 2018 and has been responsible for more than 219 million of BTS's five billion streams.[27]

The ARMYs are pretty fast, too, as they are often able to rack up views on the band's new releases within a few hours. BTS's music video for "Boy with Luv" amassed 75.6 million views in 24 hours, as announced by YouTube's Twitter account. "It is the most-viewed 24-hour debut in YouTube's history," the video streaming platform confirmed. Previously, BTS's video for "Idol" heaped up a total of 43.2 million views in 24 hours, beating the record previously held by Taylor Swift.

If that's not proof enough of their immense might, in 2017, the ARMYs rallied together online to request that American retailers, one of the biggest of which is Target, to stock their shelves with BTS's new albums. One fan in the US tweeted the idea, tagging Target and BTS's official Twitter, with the hashtag #BTSinTarget. Within hours, Target received an overload of tweets from fans all over America asking for the group's albums to be stocked in their branches across the United States. The same pattern of requests flooded toward other retailers like Walmart and Amazon. The brands listened. Target, recognizing the potential of a huge audience's attention, replied with: "These 'Fun Boys' are on 'Fire' now. We'll share your request to carry their albums with our buyers."[28]

"We aren't the representatives for K-pop," the band said at the Grammy U SoundChecks forum in Chicago. "We can't define or say what it is, but these days, thanks to social media and fans, we're lucky to have the opportunity to share our words with the world."[29]

Solidifying their title as "social media kings," BTS has won Billboard's Top Social Award for three consecutive years, with ARMYs proving this further by tweeting the hashtag #BTSBBMAS more than 300 million times. In his acceptance speech after the group won the Top Duo/Group award at the 2019 BBMAs, RM said, "Still can't believe that we're here on this stage with so many great artists. You know, this is only possible because of the little things we share, the BTS, and ARMY power. We're still the same boys from six years ago, we still have the same dreams, let's keep dreaming the best dreams together."

CHAPTER 4

THE BTS LIVE
PERFORMANCE EXPERIENCE

BTS captivated the audience when they performed "DNA" at the 2017 American Music Awards at Microsoft Theater on November 19, 2017 in Los Angeles, California.

BTS MEMBER V HAD AN UNFORGETTABLE moment right after their record-breaking concert on May 4 and 5, 2019 at the Rose Bowl Stadium in Pasadena, California, which has held the performances of many legendary artists. The venue where they kicked off their "Love Yourself: Speak Yourself" tour, which holds over 90,000 seats, was sold out.

"That sensation can't be understood without standing on that stage, but because of that performance, all my pressures and worries blew away. The emotions, fervor, ARMY's passion that completely surpassed my imagination," V shared candidly in a Japanese magazine interview. "I received it all and went back to the hotel, and cried alone in my bed. I've never cried that many happy tears [as I did] that night. I fell asleep though, so my eyes were swollen when I woke up.

When everyone at the Rose Bowl turned on their smartphone lights, I felt like I was watching stars in space. In that moment I thought of how the members were watching the same scenery with the same feeling, which I felt when I made eye contact with them, and I got even more moved," he said wistfully.[30]

While listening to the band's music and watching them on screen might tug the viewers' hearts, seeing them perform live in the flesh is an entirely sublime experience for fans. This is why fans wouldn't want to miss the chance of being in the same space as the group when the opportunity comes.

BTS has sold more than 299,770 tickets for their US stadium tours so far, raking in a staggering $44 million from concerts in three cities—the Rose Bowl in Pasadena, Chicago's Soldier Field, and New Jersey's MetLife Stadium, according to Billboard Boxscore. Their tour in São Paolo, London, and Paris added another $35 million for a combined $78.9 million and 606,409 tickets sold, according to Billboard. The figure surpassed the previous ticket sales records by top pop artists including Taylor Swift, U2, Beyonce, Jay-Z, Eminem, and Rihanna.[31]

Another feather in the band's cap is a sold-out show at Wembley Stadium, the largest concert stage in the UK, where legendary acts like Queen, Michael Jackson, the Rolling Stones, and Adele have headlined. On October 11, 2019, BTS became the first K-pop act to hold a solo stadium concert in Saudi Arabia at the King Fahd International Stadium. With the early 2020 announcement of the upcoming Map of the Soul Tour, BTS is likely to continue performing groundbreaking shows in the near future.

BTS performed on *Jimmy Kimmel Live!* on November 15, 2017 in Los Angeles, California with fans waving ARMY Bombs, the group's official fan lightsticks.

But this is not just about the ticket sales. For ARMYs, it's about making memories with BTS. The venues where BTS have played were filled with the light of ARMYs who held up the "ARMY Bomb"—the band's official lightsticks, which are connected via Bluetooth—and waved them in the air, forming a constellation-like scene of glowing lights. The audience screamed in one chorus. They sang along to each song in Korean. They held up handmade posters with the members' names. Loud waves of applause could be heard from the start to end. It was as much as a group effort for the ARMYs at it was for BTS.

Rachel Matthews of the *Daily Telegraph* called it "the bizarre and beautiful world of BTS fandom" as she observed fans who queued for twenty-eight hours outside the London's O2 where BTS was set to perform. She notes that while it is a mixture of a bewildering and amazing sight, there's a "generous spirit and sense of community which pervades the BTS universe. Positivity is everywhere."[32]

The members were also completely stunned at the turnouts, and their feelings about the ARMYs were mutual.

"Wembley holds huge significance," Suga told reporters at a press conference before their first show at the 90,000-capacity venue. "As a singer, there are some dream stages.

BTS performs "Boy with Luv" featuring chart-topping singer Halsey during the 2019 Billboard Music Awards.

Since I was young, when I watched Queen at Live Aid, I have dreamed of performing here. I couldn't sleep last night, thinking that I am performing at Wembley.[33]

"Even if there is a language barrier, once the music starts, people react pretty much the same wherever we go," he added. "It feels like the music really brings us together."

The members often give credit where it is due—to their devoted fans who not only help raise their record-breaking numbers but also lift their spirits. "I think we were able to achieve such good results because we were with our fans. It's not something we could have done alone. I don't think we're the only ones involved, [because] we're doing it together with our fans," Jin said at the Grammy U talk via a translator.

Jimin chimed in: "We give energy to our audience members and listeners, but we also draw energy from them." While J-Hope told *Time*, "We are truly honored, and thankful to our fans. Our hearts haven't changed much. As artists who love performing, we will enjoy it and do our best."

When RM uttered the words to the rest of the members, "We are making history," he was probably aware that each triumph will not only be written in their personal histories, but also in pop culture history in general. And if there's anything that these numbers are telling us, it's that BTS is making it count.

"Our music and performance receiving so much love from so many people around the world is proof that the language and borderlines in music are diminishing, and we hope that we can continue to remove those barriers," the band said at the Grammy forum. "We always try to communicate with the audience on stage. Although the venue has grown in scale, we will continue to pour our passion and energy as we always do."

CHAPTER 5

K-POP CALLS FOR CHANGE

BTS in their early 2013–2014 showcases and events in Seoul.
The band arrived on the scene at the time when K-pop fans
were clamoring for something new and real.

You can call me artist

You can call me idol
Or any other something you come up with
I don't care
I'm proud of it
I'm free
No more irony
For I was always myself

Point your fingers, I don't care at all
No matter what your reason for blaming me is
I know what I am
I know what I want
I never gon' change
I never gon' trade

What you keep babbling about
I do what I do, so mind your own business
You can't stop me lovin' myself
                    — **BTS, "Idol"**[34]

THE MORE YOU DIG INTO THE PHENOMENON THAT is BTS and how they came to be, the more you will find yourself falling into the rabbit hole of their fandom and getting swept away by their magic.

Now that we have explored, but by no means exhausted, the achievements of BTS, it is at this point crucial to ask: How did they reach the top? Who are the members of BTS and what is it about them that captivated the world? How did they go from aspiring idols to inspiring leaders of K-pop music, and perhaps, beyond? But to get there we need to go back to the very beginning: the fundamentals of Korean pop culture and

what it means to be a K-pop idol.

K-pop mixes a variety of music styles such as EDM, hip-hop, pop, and electronic. What makes it stand out, however, is the whole package with which it comes: the psychedelic music videos, colorful costumes, catchy tunes, synchronized dance, and wholesome image of the stars. It's a whole world of its own.

Many other Korean groups and solo artists before BTS have enjoyed immense popularity both in their home country and internationally. Since the late '90s and early 2000s, K-pop has branched out of South Korea and into its Asian neighbors, with Korean-language music and dramas entering millions of homes through radio and TV, and the stars acting as ambassadors of South Korea. *Hallyu,* which literally means "Korean wave," is a term used to describe the global popularity of different forms of Korean entertainment, culture, food, and travel. Part of the boom in the country's tourism can be credited to K-drama stars, with travelers from some other countries choosing South Korea as their destination after watching Korean dramas and films. From 2016 to 2017, the Korea Tourism Organization polled 3,199 people who visited the country with reservations for flights only or for flights and lodgings. 55.6 percent of travelers from China, Japan, the United States, Hong Kong, Taiwan, Thailand, Malaysia, and Singapore picked South Korea after watching TV dramas and films.[35] Meanwhile, in a 2018 report by Korean Foundation for International

Cultural Exchange, it was estimated that *Hallyu* exports accounted for $9.48 billion, with cultural contents such as games, music, and films accounting for $4.42 billion.[36]

In the early 2000s, K-pop started eyeing a much bigger, and consequently more challenging, market: America. One artist was able to crack the elusive US market in 2006. Dubbed as a "worldstar" due to his huge international following, Rain, a Korean solo singer and actor, was able to perform two shows at Madison Square Garden in New York. He also starred in two Hollywood films, the Wachowskis-directed *Speed Racer*, and *Ninja Assassin*, in which he took on the lead role. In 2011, he was voted as the Most Influential Person of the Year by *Time*'s highly anticipated 100 Poll. Rain is perhaps one of the leading trailblazers of K-pop—like many other acts such as TVXQ, BoA, Wondergirls, Big Bang, and Girls' Generation—who have "gone global" by navigating the tricky Western waters and eventually opening the doors for the next generation of K-pop stars. They first began catering to immigrants who longed for culture from back home to making the Western audience take notice. Eight years later, BTS would also make the list of *Time*'s Most Influential People of 2019, after claiming the top spot in the magazine's "Next Generation Leaders" in 2018 and being featured on the cover.

K-pop has grown so much over the past decades, and everyone wants a piece of the multibillion-dollar music export economy.

Much of these K-pop stars' success can be attributed to the entertainment agencies' well-placed system and machinery that springs from "idol trainee culture," where boys and girls as young as 10 years old audition to enter intense studio training in music, dance, acting, hosting, and many other valuable entertainment skills. This means that by the time that they become K-pop idols, they would have worked really hard for so many years. And their story of growth, passion, and dedication—aside from their catchy songs, highly stylized choreography, and impeccable good looks—are what appeals to fans. This is as much culturally rooted as it is business. Koreans believe that talent—though for some lucky ones is innate while others are simply "born with it"—can be honed and developed. The general attitude of idealism, self-reflection, and ultimately of "perfecting oneself" practiced within the K-pop industry, is, in many ways, embedded in Confucianism and the traditional hierarchy of the Korean society.

Lee Yong-doo, president of the Advanced Center for Korean Studies, explained that, "Confucian values have been rooted in Korean culture so deeply over the past 2,500 years that they have become the cultural genes of the Korean people."[37] This Confucian belief system, tradition, and religion is difficult to extract from the K-pop ecosystem, which subscribes to its core teachings of "the rectification of the mind" and "self-cultivation."[38]

As for following the Korean hierarchical system, the entertainment agencies are equivalent to the K-pop idols' home, their labelmates as siblings, while the CEO assumes the role of a father or mother figure. That is why the "Big 3" agencies in Korea—SM, YG, and JYP Entertainment—formed umbrella names for the recording artists namely: SM Town, YG Family, and JYP Nation. The head of the "family" is treated with utmost respect and his or her word is law.

But here is where it gets more complicated. Some pop star hopefuls often sign so-called "slave contracts" that run for as long as ten to fifteen years, with parents often giving consent for their kids to live in dorms so they can focus on training while the agency takes care of their schooling and living arrangements in the process. As the young people grow up and enhance their skills, they are evaluated regularly until they are deemed ready to debut. More than half of the trainees will not make it—and if they do, it will entail years of being bound to the company with no guarantee of success or financial reward.

Everything is controlled: their style of dress, image, personality, and private lives. There's a reason why they are called "idols," after all, as they need to embody what the nation considers ideal.

"If you go to the agency, every young trainee will give you a very polite bow and there are notices with the company rules on the walls to remind them how to behave," Mark Russell, an expert on the K-pop industry, told the BBC.[39] Dating or even having close platonic relationships with the opposite sex, which may be misinterpreted by the public, is prohibited. "It's possibly comparable to the situation in the 1940s in the US when film studios had huge control over their movie stars but even then, they may have been encouraged not to date or marry but there was less coercion," Asia Bureau Chief of *Billboard* magazine Rob Schwartz added.

Former Crayon Pop girl-group member Way testified to the "dark side of the K-pop industry" when she shared with media content company Asian Boss her experience of her agency label's unforgiving methods. "I had to go on a strict diet. We practiced dance all day and would get back to the dorms after midnight, but had to go to practice every day at 4AM," she recalled. "Dating is a taboo. To keep us from dating, the company took our phones and forbid us from going out. It was so strict that we couldn't even meet our families."[40] She added, "I want young people who desire to become K-Pop stars to see the hard work and sacrifice that goes behind it. I hope they won't aspire to become idols by just looking at the glamorous side."

Similarly, former K-pop idol Prince Mak lamented in a YouTube video that even after debuting, some stars commonly work for as long as eighteen hours a day and only earn two dollars—that is, "if you're lucky." But he went on to add that it is an amazing experience, as long as one is clear about its downsides and if that idol aspirant is doing it for the love of singing and dancing in front of a large audience. "What I do know from experience is that you can be famous and not make any money," he stressed.[41]

Not only do these music labels have hands-on control over their idols' physical image, they are also cautious about their opinions on particular matters. Discussions about political and social issues, injustice, sexuality, mental health, and other sensitive themes are highly guarded. Anyone who violates the agencies' rigid standards and rules is subjected to harsh public criticism, disciplinary actions, or worse, eviction from the company.

In more recent news, it was reported that the South Korean government has been cracking down on K-pop agencies that are allegedly involved in illegal practices.

But while the conversation on the oppressive side of K-pop is extremely important, we shouldn't generalize. It is true that this idol incubation system may have caused negative impacts on the industry and its artists. However, it is also necessary to note that this is not only exclusive to South Korea and certainly not only applicable to K-pop. Adam White of the *Telegraph* referred to the Mickey Mouse Club as "America's version of a pre-teen K-Pop boot camp," with equal risks of making or breaking the careers and psyche of young kids hoping to become stars. "It is not an enormous reach to suggest that the mainstream media's endless regurgitation of 'the dark side' of K-pop is a means to 'other' a culture that is visually different than our own. Particularly when there's truly not much of a difference between the abuses that occur in the Korean music industry and within the halls of Western labels and recording studios."

Despite its controversies and inadequacies, the genre has produced a great number of fulfilled artists who continue to make music that inspires new generations of fans. With the public becoming more aware of the issues and authorities taking heed, it will only be a matter of time before change takes place.

One thing we can take away from this is that there is a growing vexation among different entities: the artists who are being exploited by their agencies and the majority of audiences who are now starting to distrust the whole system. Fans are also yearning for authenticity, a new generation of K-pop idols who are not only entertainers but also artists who open meaningful conversations, create new experiences, and inspire their fans.

CHAPTER 6

STEPPING OUTSIDE THE NORM:
THE RISE OF THE ROGUE PRODUCER

THE MEMBERS OF BTS HAVE ALSO STARTED AS trainees and considered the head of their agency their mentor, boss, and in some ways, their father figure. But what then, makes them different from other K-pop stars? This is where Bang Si-hyuk, nicknamed "Hitman Bang," comes in.

"People were very curious. They knew him as someone who originally wrote hit ballads, but how did he pop out of nowhere?" RM, the first member to be signed with the company, said in a clip from "Good Insight," which showed behind-the-scenes footage of BTS.[42]

Bang started as a producer under mega-entertainer and CEO of JYP Entertainment, Park Jin-young, who was behind the success of g.o.d., Rain, Wondergirls, 2PM, GOT7, Twice, and other famous K-pop acts.

Park once stated in an interview that twenty years ago, JYP Entertainment consisted of only three employees: himself, Bang Si-hyuk, and an employee on the accounting team. Bang was given the moniker "Hitman" for having produced and written a number of hit songs, and especially for his extensive work with g.o.d., which helped to make them one of Korea's best-selling and most popular boy bands of the early 2000s.[43]

Meanwhile, the certified hit-maker credits Park as someone "who has taught me everything about producing from A to Z." He would later part ways with JYP and build his own company, Big Hit Entertainment, in 2005.

Having learned music producing from the best and having seen the ups and downs of managing K-pop groups, Bang felt a need for change. But more particularly, what he felt was "anger" and "rage" toward mediocrity and unfairness in society, which he says can also be seen in the Korean music industry.

In South Korea, politeness in public rhetoric is expected and it is often required for celebrities or personalities to speak from scripts that fall on the "safe" side. But Bang was different.

In his 2019 commencement address to graduates of Seoul National University, his alma mater, he revealed his "dissatisfaction" with the passive attitude and mindless conformity of the Korean society as a whole.[44]

"There are so many compromises in this world. Many are complacent about change, even when there are better ways to do things for many reasons, from not wanting to stick out, not wanting to cause trouble, or perhaps because it was always done this way. But by nature, I can't just compromise. When it comes to my work, and even with things that are not directly related to me, I will complain if the best efforts are not made in any situation. And if the situation doesn't improve despite that, I become furious," he said with conviction.

"I was angry for the complacency of picking the second best instead of the best, or the custom and practice of settling for mediocrity for many different reasons. But above all, I was most unhappy with the situations facing the music industry. This industry was absolutely unreasonable, unfair, and irrational. As I chose music as my career, getting to know about this world, my anger got bigger. It felt as if the music, which I loved the most in the world, was treated unfairly and is being used by this world."

He also spoke openly about the lack of integrity of the K-pop idol culture, which many of his colleagues often omit in their interviews and speeches. "Many music industry personnel are still ashamed of saying they are part of this industry, due to the industry's corrupt practices, unfairness and undervaluation by the society. Many young people still regard a music company as paying pittance for hard work."

This anger fueled his goals when he set up his company, Big Hit. He made it his mission to fight the ills of the music industry and envisioned a company that "spreads good influence in the society, and especially gives positive influence to our customers who are young people, helping them create their own world view."

He used this kind of approach and mindset when he began conceptualizing the band that would be known as BTS. Instead of grooming idols that seem like puppets following the agency's every order, he wanted to find a balance between "toughness" and "sincerity," where members are recognized for their inner strength against society's pressures and openness to helping others, which reflected the band's original name "Bulletproof Boy Scouts." He wanted to create an approachable group who can fill the roles of both a friend and hero to the youth. "I didn't want them to be false idols,"

Bang added. "I wanted to create BTS that could become a close friend."

Necessity is the mother of invention, as the adage says, and the precarious environment of the K-pop industry opened the doors for BTS's arrival into the scene. "Many fans in Korea are discontent with labeling BTS as K-Pop acts because they think they are more or beyond K-pop. Particularly when the K-Pop world in general is mired in very severe scandals involving sex and drug scandals, rape allegations, and whatnot," Suk-Young Kim, a professor of critical studies at the University of California, Los Angeles, told CNBC.[45]

"I recently came across a company document from [2012], the year before BTS debuted, in which we were debating what kind of idol group to create. It said, 'What kind of hero is the youth of today looking for? Not someone who dogmatically preaches from above. Rather, it seems like they need a hero who can lend them a shoulder to lean on, even without speaking a single word.'"[46]

As for managing the career and "image" of BTS members, Bang challenged the traditional conventions of strict contracts and authoritarian upbringing of talents. He gave them freedom to write their own songs, and ultimately, the autonomy to have a say in everything: costumes, choreography, music videos, and performances.

BTS and the future groups in his company are allowed to be themselves and have a voice. Finally, the idols who were once expected to be flawless and pure can embrace their "human" side: young people who are vulnerable, unsure, and unpretentious. They make mistakes and learn from them. They, just like many other people their age, have worries about the future, insecurities about themselves, and are still grappling with finding their place in the world.

Bang resolved to make a band that was simply real. "I didn't restrict them," the producer said. "When I first met the members, the goal wasn't for them to become international artists. It hadn't been long since they'd come to Seoul, and our company also wasn't in the mainstream. I just thought that I could make something meaningful together with these guys."

RM recalled, "When we had our conversation with Mr. Bang when we first started out, he always emphasized that we should sing about our own experiences, our own thoughts, our own feelings. So, that has always been at the center of the music that we made."[47]

Bang made the possibilities for BTS's music repertoire to be endless. He shared, "Since we decided that BTS would be singers who told the truth about reality, we said, 'Let's talk about pain, and let's say that instead of just living passively, we should work hard to overcome obstacles. Whether we win or lose, it's having dreams that makes us young.'"

Liberating BTS from the constricting norms of K-pop culture is only part of his bigger plan: "I feel happy when I can be part of changing paradigms of the music industry, help develop it, and take part in improving the quality of life of the professionals in this industry."

As for being called "father" to the group? He says he doesn't quite like it. "The idea [of me being the father of BTS] makes the group an object, not the subject, and that's against my philosophy. Also, I'm not married," he said in an interview with *Korea JoongAng Daily*.

CHAPTER 7

REVOLUTIONARY K-POP STARS ARE BORN

Shine, dream, smile
Oh let us light up the night
We shine in our own ways
Shine, dream, smile
Oh let us light up the night
We shine just the way we are
Tonight

— BTS, "Mikrokosmos"[48]

The members of BTS are from different backgrounds, with RM hailing from Seoul and the rest from hometowns in far-flung regions in South Korea. Not one of them knew that they would one day become superstars with millions of fans all over the world. But they did, however, have one thing in common: "We came together with a dream to write, dance and produce music that reflects our musical backgrounds as well as our life values of acceptance, vulnerability and being successful," said RM in an interview with *Time*.

They may be in a group, but they also have their own individual talents, personalities, charms, and idiosyncrasies, and as their song says, they "shine in their own ways." Here, get to know the members in depth, beginning with the first member to sign with Big Hit: RM.

KIM NAM JOON AKA RM

Leader, Main Rapper

C'mon y'all, moonchild, moonchild
That's how it's supposed to be
Yeah all this pain and all this sorrow
That's our destiny, see?
You and my life was like this
We gotta dance in the rain
Dance in the pain
Even though we crash down
We gon' dance in the plane
We need the scenery, the night, more than anybody
Only I could console myself, not nobody else
It's okay to shed the tears
But don't you tear yourself
— **RM, "MOONCHILD"**[49]

WITH FEWER THAN THIRTY EMPLOYEES UNDER HIS new company and with little budget, Bang Si-hyuk said he was still figuring out his next steps—until one teenager set his plans in motion. "Back in 2010, I got a call from a friend telling me there's this kid who's got incredible rapping skills," he recalled in an interview. Soon after he got wind of this teenager who was blowing up in the underground rap scene, he decided to see for himself. Kim Nam Joon—a student whose original lyrics, flow, and confidence on stage belied his young age—blew him away. He had skills that were also recognized by professional rappers in the mainstream scene even before he was discovered.

Bang's initial plan was to form a hip-hop team around this prodigy. But Bang changed his direction: "The idol music, as I saw it, was all about partying and living the moment," he said, and instead he "wanted a new group that talks about real life difficulties experienced by millennials."[50]

> **"I have my persona, RM, and I have my other persona, Kim Nam Joon, a normal 25-year-old in Korea, and we have to keep those two personas and two names alive."**
> **—RM**

Kim Nam Joon would adopt the stage name "Rap Monster," and later simply, RM. In Korea, the word "monster" does not pertain to a frightening creature; rather, it connotes some kind of genius or someone who's incredibly good at what he or she does. "[The name] came from a song that I made from like, 2012, there was some phrase like Rap Monster, and I thought it was so cool. But as I grow up, and as I came to America, I think it felt like too much. So I just abbreviated it to RM, and it could symbolize many things. It could have more spectrums to it," RM explained. When asked what his name means to him right now, he replied, "I don't know, like, 'Real Me' or something."[51]

RM is the designated leader of the group whenever they have promotional activities or interviews outside of South Korea, as he is the only member who can speak fluent English.

He taught himself by watching the TV series *Friends* over and over until he got comfortable with the language. But what makes him even more special is that he really does have a profound love for words. From a young age, he had a penchant for reading poetry and started writing poems himself, which he would upload to an online poetry website. At school, he was recognized as a top student and received awards for his writing. It was even reported that he scored in the top one percent of the nation in the university entrance examinations for language, math, foreign language, and social studies, and he has an IQ of 148.[52]

People around RM expected him to pursue a literary career in the future. What changed it all, however, was the moment when he first heard the song "Fly" from renowned South Korean hip-hop group, Epik High.

From writing poetic lines to composing song lyrics, RM dabbled in playing with words. At the young age of thirteen, he began rapping with an underground group called DaeNamHyup. He also participated in small concerts with underground rappers, one of whom was Zico, who would later join the group Block B and become one of the most sought-after rappers in Korea.

It was another industry player who would bring RM to the spotlight. Rapper Sleepy happened to attend an underground crew audition where RM, who at that time was only in his third year of middle school, was participating.

Sleepy shared, "I heard that Rap Monster was the first one to be chosen as a member of BTS. But I wonder if it would have happened if it hadn't been for me. I'm proud that I was the one who discovered him. I got his phone number, called Big Hit Entertainment, and asked them to take a look."

It turned out Sleepy's instincts were correct. "Recently, I opened up a hard drive that I'd used in the old days," he continued. "I found some raps that Rap Monster had done before his debut, back when he used the name 'Runch Randa.' I have about ten songs. He's gotten to where he is now because he's good."[53]

By good he refers to RM's mastery of composing lines that are filled with wit and hidden meanings.

Rap Monster, like my name
I can eat up any kind of beat like a monster
I'm loyal to my name, guys come here,
   take a preview
I put a twist to being an idol
Haha, *hyungs*[54] who only had hip-hop pride
Told me it'd be impossible but
Look carefully, I place a period after impossible
I'm possible, now are we all set, boy?
                     — RM's verse in
          "We Are Bulletproof Pt. 2"[55]

RM mentions his major influences in his songs, particularly Eminem, Garion, and Epik High. But instead of following their music styles, his compositions always have hints of philosophical teachings or stories from books that he has read. A self-professed bookworm, RM has perused the books of prolific authors like Albert Camus, J. D. Salinger, Haruki Murakami, and Hermann Hesse, among many others.[56] These writers have inspired some of BTS's most iconic music videos, and it was RM who pitched in some of the most profound ideas.

On camera, RM is known as the leader or "president" of the group, but off camera and at home, he is simply a friend and a brother to the members. "He takes responsibility for bad things by himself and shares good things with us," V shared, saying he respects RM as "the bridge connecting us and the company. It must have stressed him and hurt him a lot, but he doesn't show it at all. He takes it all on himself."

RM is often admired by fans for having wisdom at such a young age, as he often speaks using metaphors and analogies. Fans

feel he does this ever so spontaneously and without a smidgen of pretentiousness, and often refer fondly to him as "the philosopher" or "the sexy brain" of the group. "RM is extremely self-reflective, sophisticated and philosophical considering his age," Bang said.

"Life is more beautiful knowing that we've taken a loan on death. Even light is treasured more when there is darkness,"[57] RM says in one of his musings on life. As for the growing pains and fading of youth, he discussed via a solo V Live session what he learned from a teacher: "In your twenties if you have so many thoughts, that's like branches on a tree. If my brain is a tree, there are so many branches: there's sadness, there's

desperation, devastation, there's happiness, hope, everything. But when you get old, it gets cut and when it gets some shape of a tree, we have to feel pain and we have to experience many things. If you've got so many branches in your twenties, and you feel sad and sometimes get lost, someday, you will finally be a really beautiful tree in your thirties and forties. Sometimes, I meet good and cool old people, they've got the attitude like they've experienced so many things, so maybe we can one day have that."[58]

In RM's song "Do You," he scathingly spoke about his disdain for self-help books, being trapped in labels, and following conventions. By the end of the song, he urges his listeners to just "Do you."

I hate self-help books more than anything
   in the world
Bullsh*t telling us to do this or that
They have no backbone and believe other's
   words
So that bullsh*t is a best seller
What do those guys know about you
Your dreams, your hobbies, can they
   understand?
If you look less at wits, there are a lot of
   things that change
You were born as a hero, why are you trying
   to become a slave?
"Because it hurts, it's youth"
That kind of definition is the biggest problem
. . .
Just wear what you want, how you want to,
   that's swag, that's it
(whoa!) if you follow the trends that's good
(whoa!) if you're totally different that's good
Just you yourself is hood, originally
   everything from the beginning
There was nothing right or wrong, just that
   various things are different
                    — **RM, "Do You"**[59]

Aside from his incredible work with BTS,
RM has released solo efforts in straightforward
mixtapes that drew more insights from his
deeply personal experiences. His solo EP
project titled *Mono* debuted to rave reviews.
"It's a decidedly melodic, genreless effort by a
polyvalent pop star who spent years establishing
himself as a 'traditional' hip-hop lyricist. It features
fleshed out ideas of solitude, depression, and
the search for meaning," a reviewer wrote in an
article for the music website DJ Booth. They

went on further to say that "RM is a K-Pop Icon
and a Hip-Hop legend."[60]

Another telling review came from NME,
an online media company based in London:
"Last year, the rapper took to a BTS fan forum
to describe himself as a fan of 'that moment
where twilight and evening transitions to night,
and the moment when dawn transitions to
morning.' 'Mono' sounds like it was created with
those moments in mind. This is a soundtrack
for walking the streets, contemplating life and
working through your thoughts as the sky
changes gears. It's atmospheric and reflective,
and shows his impressive growth since its
predecessor's release."[61]

His lyrics show his struggle in finding a
balance between himself as "RM" and "Kim
Nam Joon."

But why do I feel lonely?
I feel so lonely when I'm with me
. . .
My ideal and what is reality
They're so far, far away
But I still want to cross that two bridges
To reach myself
To the real me
                    — **RM, "Uhgood"**[62]

But as RM matured over the years and
learned lessons along the way, he was able
to reconcile that he can have both identities,
one onstage and one away from it. "When
you grow up and when the night comes and
the sun is down, a man's shadow becomes
longer," RM explained in an interview about
the group's album, *Persona*.

"So if my height gets higher, the shadow becomes longer. Sometimes it is too much and too hard and too big for us, but to live and survive as an artist and a human and a person who trusts and loves themselves, we need to be friends with the shadows.

Our new album is called *Persona*. I have my persona, RM, and I have my other persona, Kim Nam Joon, a normal 25-year-old in Korea, and we have to keep those two personas and two names alive."

MIN YOON-GI AKA SUGA, AGUST D
Lead Rapper

You could be my new thang
I'm different from the *hyungs*
That ignore their duties
An uprising of celebrities
Damn only strong ones can mess with me
I'm the thorn in the eyes of those *hyungs*
Who have no chances of becoming successful
Honestly, "Ssaihanuwar" is embarrassing
We sell 500,000 copies a year
My size is different to fit in the K-pop category
. . .
A to the G to the U to STD
I'm D boy because I'm from D
I'm the crazy guy, the lunatic on beat
— Agust D (Suga), "Agust D"[63]

HAILING FROM DAEGU, A BIG CITY KNOWN FOR ITS unforgiving humid subtropical climate and distinct character, is Min Yoon-gi, a young man whose passion burns as intensely as his hometown's weather. "I'm the crazy guy, the lunatic on beat," he raps fiercely, with unexpectedly frank and aggressive lines that somewhat contradict his sweet, boyish good looks.

Suga was quite unlike others who would spend time with friends from school, play games, and study like teens his age would normally do. From early on, he would pore over rap albums and listen to them endlessly, much to the disapproval of his parents. He found himself looking for a way to express himself through rap by joining the underground hip-hop crew D-Town, under the stage name "Gloss."

At seventeen, Suga got a job at a recording studio and eventually gained a strong interest in arranging songs. In time, his name got popular as the wunderkind who could spit fiery rhymes with his own self-composed beats. Even older underground rappers enlisted his help in producing tracks, with rapper Reflow working with him on the song, "Who Am I?"

"I used to work as a studio engineer while composing and performing at the same time in Daegu," Suga shared. "But there was no one [there] when I performed. 50 people was a lot. I lost money every day, I didn't even have enough money to eat after performing." He also shared that once he only had two dollars in his pocket, which is the price of a bowl of noodles or a bus ticket. "I had to choose only one. If I wanted to eat, I wouldn't be able to take the bus."

But even though Daegu is one of the biggest cities in Korea, the young maven wanted to take his music to the next level and make his songs heard through platforms that have a wider reach. He then happened to see a flyer from Big Hit Entertainment, with details about an open talent search event called "Hit It."

Yoon-gi won second place and expressed his desire to join the company as a record

producer. Bang Si-hyuk, seeing more potential in him, decided to include him in the boy band he was planning to create, and see if he would fit in. Yoon-gi didn't have any background in dancing, and had this "rough around the edges" image that was so unlike the typical clean-cut, boy-next-door looks of successful idols. But more than "fitting in," Yoon-gi stood out for his mysterious charm and skill that enabled him to master singing and dancing, collecting new skills like a sponge.

Bang came up with the stage name "Suga," short for the word *sugar*, which describes his sweet personality and pale complexion. The rapper revealed to *Cuvism* magazine that, although he suggested to use his old stage name at first, he liked the ring of his new name because it reminded him of his position of "shooting guard" in basketball. "I came up to Seoul because I wanted to let many people hear my music, so BTS's achievements feels like a miracle," he said in the *BTS Wings Concept Book*.[64]

In 2016, Suga released his own impassioned mixtape called *Agust D*, a mix of his name spelled backward and the letter *D*, which paid tribute to his hometown, Daegu. What caught critics' ears about his lyrics was his pure honesty and raw emotions, with songs that boldly discussed sensitive issues such as the "reality of depression, OCD and social phobia that has plagued Suga between the time he left his hometown to pursue his dream in Seoul and the anguish he's felt about selling out."[65]

On the other side of the famous idol rapper
Stands my weak self, it's a bit dangerous
Depression, OCD
They keep coming back again from time to time
Hell no perhaps that might be my true self
Damn huh feeling estranged in reality
The conflict with ideal, my head hurts
Around the age of 18, I developed social anxiety
Right, that was when my mind was
   gradually polluted

Right, that performance day
Which I don't remember very well
The day I confronted myself
When I hid inside the bathroom
Because I was scared of people

I've exchanged my youth for success
And that monster demands for more wealth
At times it puts a collar on my neck
To ruin and swallow me with greed
Some try to shut my mouth and say
I should swallow this forbidden fruit
I don't want it
They want me to leave this garden
        — Agust D (Suga), "The Last"[66]

One review read, "What makes it so unique is that different people from different parts of the world resonate with his music. Suga's storytelling execution in the music he creates tears down the barrier of censoring and sugarcoating."[67] Meanwhile, *Billboard* commended it for being "intense in its vulnerability," citing Suga's courage to tell the message of "the contradictory desire for the reality of life to be nothing more than a dream

while at the same time urging his army of listeners to dream on." This is reflected in one of Suga's lyrics in "The Last": "My fans, keep your head high with pride."

After releasing his solo mixtape, he was able to finally heave a sigh of relief. "Mr. Bang told me I've become much brighter and asked where that person full of wrath from before had gone. Thinking about how many idols can have this chance, I'm making music in a very good environment. BTS, Agust D or a human named Min Yoon-gi, it all comes from the same person, so if I put in my real stories, many people can listen and relate to it," he said in the *Wings Concept Book*.

As of this writing, the Korea Music Copyright Association attributes over eighty-four songs to Suga as a songwriter and composer, including works with prestigious Korean artists. He coproduced "Eternal Sunshine" by Epik High, "Wine" by Suran, and "We Don't Talk Together" by Heize. Some of his tracks won music awards, including best R&B track of the year at the 2017 Melon Music Awards for the song "Wine."

With his extensive credits as a producer, Suga was appointed as a full member of the Korea Music Copyright Association (KOMCA) in 2018, alongside some of Korea's most respected artists like BoA, IU, and Tiger JK, among others. Fellow members RM and J-Hope were also promoted as full-fledged members of KOMCA at the beginning of 2020. According to *Soompi*, this role is important since "KOMCA is a nonprofit copyright collective with the objective of improving music culture in Korea through protecting the rights of copyright holders and ensuring ease of use for listeners. It is a respected organization that was founded in 1964, and it maintains a database of copyrighted works and their producers."[68]

After the success of his first solo effort, Suga released "D-2," which featured the title track "Daechwita," which refers to a Korean traditional genre of music. It topped Billboard's World Albums Chart, while the single is praised by fans and critics for its bold lyrics and Suga's pride for his roots.

For Suga, music will always be something that enables him to show his emotions and, ultimately, connect with people. He said in the *BTS Wings Concept Book*, "I don't think I live an ordinary life. I started making music since I was young and left home at a young age too. I don't show [my emotions] much usually, basically not at all. But I always live hoping someone would know it. Through music I convey messages like 'It's okay to fall,' or 'It's okay to get hurt.' I just want to make music that gives people hope."

JUNG HO-SEOK AKA J-HOPE

Main Dancer, Rapper, Sub Vocalist

I remember me from that time
When the dry ground lit me ablaze
I ran looking at the blue sky
I wanted to fly in that airplane

It's still not believable to me
That this Gwangju kid could get wrapped
  up in flight
From my place in this high, high dream
I'm flying above the beautiful world
Every time I ride
The nerves I felt before our first Japan trip
I still think of them
That was what launched my dream
That was what made "now"
Everywhere
Now I'm an issue man, when the flash goes off
I put my blessing on a safe arrival
God bless

— J-Hope, "Airplane"[69]

JUNG HO-SEOK, THE THIRD BTS MEMBER TO release a mixtape, welcomes us to his world colored with pop, EDM, funk, and lively Caribbean beats. He is known for his precise dance moves, cheerful personality, and ability to brighten up the room with his positive vibe. People around him often say that there's never a day that goes by when he doesn't greet anyone happily or flash his gleaming smile. He embodies his chosen stage name "J-Hope," which denotes more of his aim rather than a cool-sounding moniker.

"My name has the deepest meaning out of all the others in this group," J-Hope jokingly told *Time*. "You know how in Pandora's Box after everything else left, the only thing remaining was hope, right? I put 'hope' in my name to be a hopeful existence in the group. I got the 'J' from my last name, Jung. That's how I became J-Hope."

Born and raised in the South Korean city of Gwangju, J-Hope can often be found rhythmically moving to any kind of music. His love for dancing runs deep. While in school, he joined dance groups and entered local competitions where he would win top prizes. He first got his taste of popularity when he joined an underground dance team called Neuron.

It's the year 2010
My steps head to Seoul
I, who started out just loving dance
Is soon to stand on stage
Until then I combat the many pains and
    scars and prepare myself
I nurture my notion to bend rather than to break
And run for 3 years
And ignite the stars in my heart
Now see me anew
I carve 'Bangtan' into a blank page that
    means the whole world
I walk towards my brighter future
I put on a smile for the further days
                    — **J-Hope's verse in "Road/Path"**[70]

Wanting to try his luck in the K-pop scene, he first auditioned at JYP Entertainment, where he passed a few rounds until he couldn't make the final cut. Another agency close to JYP, Big Hit, would give him a chance, though, and in turn unknowingly gave him his biggest break as the main dancer and one of the rappers of BTS.

In 2018, he released *Hope World*, a seven-track mixtape that took him two years to complete. He considers it as a way to introduce himself and his "calling card to the world," while emphasizing that, "The team always comes first, so I focused on our projects as BTS and tried to make time in the hotel room, on the airplane, and whenever I could find a few minutes."[71]

> "You know how in Pandora's Box after everything else left, the only thing remaining was hope, right? I put 'hope' in my name to be a hopeful existence in the group. I got the 'J' from my last name, Jung. That's how I became J-Hope."
>
> — J-Hope

> My name is my life
> A hopeful vibe
> A positive rather than a negative type
> I live up to my name but ain't no price
> (Whoo)
> Not a romanticist
> An age without a hitch
> I enjoy curses and vulgar language,
> But I don't do that in my music
> . . .
> Say hello to my Hope World
> This is my world, my own story
> I run 20,000 leagues under the sea
> . . .
> This is style, This is mine
> The same-same kids, one body one mind Time
> To be in one body and soul
> Let's try it together, it's a submarine here
> Everyone's Aronnax, I'm Captain Nemo
>
> — J-Hope, "Hope World"[72]

While his bandmates RM and Suga often tell their personal stories in pensive, darker tones, J-Hope does so in a more playful manner. His first song "Hope World" began with sounds of splashing water, which would provide a peek of his musical style leading into the rest of the album. He was inspired by the book *Twenty Thousand Leagues Under the Sea*, which he read as a kid. He explained in his interview with *Time*, "It's an introduction to people who are brand new to [me] with me as Captain Nemo showing you around just as the submarine in the book cruised around the world's oceans. I know this might sound really corny, but I invite you to pretend to be Professor Aronnax as you listen to this song and take a journey through my world."

Vocal Media describes his work, saying, "It shows his ideals, his dreams, all the qualities and values that make him who he is. It's always impressive when an artist can be so transparent and honest in their work, and be willing to share that with millions of fans. *Hope World* is a fun listening experience that does just what J-Hope wants it to do: make people smile."[73]

In "Hope World," the rapper and dancer is coming to grips with his fame, oftentimes finding it hard to believe that a kid from the province has come this far. He elaborated further in *Time*, "I think 'making it,' as you say, means different things to different people. I was sitting in an airplane when I was writing

these verses, a first-class seat no less, and it dawned on me that I was in the airplane, in the seat and living the glorious life I'd only dreamed about when I was young, and had somehow gotten used to now. My thoughts on life haven't changed very much. But my world has gone through incredible changes. I think it was that experience of being with my fans around the world and stepping back on Korean soil that it hit me, 'Man, I think I've made it . . .' For me, the joy that I have right now and the amazing love I'm getting is how I define my success."

His mixtape is only the first of many of his solo ventures. His single "Chicken Noodle Soup" with Becky G debuted with 9.7 million streams in the US and 11,000 downloads sold in a single week in October, according to Nielsen Music and reported by Billboard.com. The song featured English, Korean, and Spanish lyrics and had a catchy dance routine that became widely viral, with the hashtag #CNSChallenge trending on social media platforms. Billboard also notes that the song is more than just a viral craze: "But perhaps even more notably than its viral appeal is the wide range of representation featured in the song (a Korean rapper, a Latinx singer, samples of a hip-hop song that honors Harlem [of the same name,

by Da Drizzle, from 2006]) and video itself (with reportedly more than 50 countries represented by the multicultural dance crew)."

Even with his apparent success with the band and as a solo performer, J-Hope remains grounded: "People know me, and I know I'm a person in the public's eye. I wanted to show that behind this public figure is an ordinary guy named Jung Ho-seok."

KIM SEOK-JIN AKA JIN
Vocalist, Visual

I'm the one I should love in this world
Shining me, precious soul of mine
I finally realized so I love me
Not so perfect but so beautiful
I'm the one I should love

I'm shaking and afraid but I keep going forward
I'm meeting the real you, hidden in the storm
Why did I want to hide my precious self like this?
What was I so afraid of?
Why did I hide my true self?
. . .

I may be a bit blunt, I may lack some things
I may not have that shy glow around me
But this is me
My arms, my legs, my heart, my soul
— **Jin, "Epiphany"**[74]

THE ELDEST MEMBER OF BTS, JIN GOT THE nickname "worldwide handsome" from local and international fans who admired his incredible good looks. Whenever he gets asked to introduce himself during interviews, he looks into the camera with a straight face and cheerfully says, "I'm worldwide handsome!"—much to the chagrin of the other members of BTS, who laugh and face-palm, while RM tries to move the conversation along to fill in the gap of slight awkwardness. This friendly banter among BTS members is common, where they often show that it's okay to be confident and poke fun at each other at the same time.

> **"I'm actually shy in front of strangers. I'm just a person. I'm merely a human who makes up this world, but when I step one foot outside, I'm treated as a 'star who was on TV.'"**
> **—JIN**

But Jin and the fans' claim aren't just mere conjecture. His "worldwide handsome face" is, in fact, proven by research.

Professional doll designer company from Czech CzDollic conducted four months of research analyzing 18,000 male faces from a total of fifty-eight countries to find the best-sculpted face in the world. Among the chosen top-ten finalists, the company received a total of 1,504,602 public votes. The winner? Kim Seok-jin from South Korea. He took the top spot along with Ravi Bhatia from India and American supermodel Sean O'Pry, who were runners-up. According to the firm, they used a three-dimensional design by sculptor Radek Schick, who explained that, "His oval features balanced symmetrically, that can be filmed from any angle and his mouth beautifully curved."[75] Meanwhile, an unnamed plastic surgeon analyzed the measurements of 269 male Asian faces and concluded that Jin's face fits the "golden ratio," a method of measurement for determining perfectly balanced features.[76]

This isn't the first time Jin has gone viral. The hashtag #thirdmemberfromtheleft trended on Twitter after the May 2017 Billboard Awards, along with #cardoorguy when a video of him getting out of the car at a red-carpet event captured everyone's attention.

But when conversations and interviews turn to a more serious note, Jin shows that he is more than just his good looks. "As the

Born in Gwacheon, Gyeonggi Province, in South Korea, Jin has always had his sights on pursuing acting. He graduated from Konkuk University in Seoul in 2011, with a degree in theater and film.[77] He was first scouted on the street by mega K-pop company SM Entertainment, which he turned down at that time thinking it was a scam. But it turned out to be a blessing in disguise when he was approached by an employee of Big Hit as he was getting off the bus.[78] He originally auditioned as an actor, but the CEO thought he could become a great addition to BTS. Without natural singing or dancing skills, Jin would train hard, with his peers and teachers recognizing his determination from the very beginning.

Proving detractors wrong about his role in the group, Jin learned how to play the piano and guitar, and helped co-write lyrics on some of BTS's albums. In 2017, Jin decided to pursue graduate studies by enrolling in Hanyang Cyber University, alongside members Jimin and V. "I've always wanted to convey various messages to the public, in ways other than music as well," Jin said in his entrance ceremony video.

oldest member, I think I experienced the world a little sooner than many people my age, so I think I am a grown-up. I just act like a kid on purpose. I feel like a grown-up when I talk to my friends and they ask for advice," he said of his age in the *BTS Now 3* magazine. And despite his playfulness and confidence on camera, he reveals, "I'm actually shy in front of strangers. I'm just a person. I'm merely a human who makes up this world, but when I step one foot outside, I'm treated as a 'star who was on TV.'"

His sensitivity and caring personality are often mentioned by the group, with RM describing him as someone like a "mom," whereas Jimin thinks he's like a "grandmother," saying he's the one most likely to give wise advice and clean up after them at home after a hard day's work.

When this night passes
I'm afraid I won't be able to see you

The utterly clear gaze
The touch I got too used to
The face that smiled at me
Will I be unable to see you again anymore?

In my every day
You are there
In your every day
I'm there
When the moon is gone
And the sun rises
The one who has been with me
Will you be gone?

— **Jin, "This Night"**[79]

In an interview, V revealed that even though Jin may always look carefree, "He really works hard. He practices in the hotel room alone until the break of dawn. When everyone's tired, he makes an effort to take care of us, heal us, and make us laugh."

Just like the other members, fame is not something that Jin can get used to easily, but he tries to keep it all in stride by "trying not to hurry things up."

"To be honest, I can't deny that I don't feel pressure. I don't think I'm the type [who's] able to handle everything. But I have my members. That's why we're able to face the world with our force," he said in a magazine interview.[80]

JEON JUNGKOOK AKA JUNGKOOK

Main Vocalist, Lead Dancer, Sub Rapper, Center, *Maknae*

The name is Jung Kook, my scale is nationwide
I pulled all-nighters at practice rooms
Instead of school, dancing and singing
While you guys partied
I gave up sleep for my dreams
> **— Jungkook's verse in "We Are Bulletproof Pt. 2"**[81]

BEING THE YOUNGEST IN ANY GROUP, PEOPLE often face similar stereotypes: young people are troublemakers because they can get away with more things, they're stubborn, or they're naive. Jungkook, the "baby" of BTS, is quite the opposite. His skills in singing and dancing often exceed expectations. For this reason, he is often dubbed as the "golden *maknae*," which is the Korean term of endearment for being the most talented and youngest, therefore an indispensable part of the group. But even when he gets countless praise from his elders and even experts in the field, he still considers himself lacking. "I'm the type to cower inside a little bit," he explained in the *BTS Wings Concept Book*.[82] "I tend to think I have a long way to go even if I dance well or think 'I can't sing,' even if they say I sing well. I would still be like that ten years later, when I practice and become someone who can really sing well. I would keep this thought even if I'm the ultimate vocalist."

Perhaps it is his humble spirit that enables him to excel in his craft. Or maybe it's his mature way of thinking. "I want to be a real adult too," he said, sharing how the older members inspire him tremendously. "I tend to have to go through something to know it. If they tell me so, I'll fix myself little by little. I'm gradually learning thanks to the *hyungs* (older brothers). Looking at the other *hyungs*, I think, 'Don't they know themselves and do well?' They can think and create something by themselves, but I still lack a lot so there's not much I can do by myself."

Would I have changed?
If I had chosen a different path
If I had stopped and looked back
What will I get to see?
At the end of this road
Where you would be standing
> **— Jungkook's verse in "Road/Path"**[83]

Coming all the way from his hometown of Busan to move to Seoul and chase his dreams as a teenager, Jungkook felt a lot of uncertainties and worries, especially competing with other talents from the big city. He first got discovered when he auditioned for a Korean reality TV show, *Superstar K*, where he bested the other contestants before finally being eliminated. But the show gave him the right exposure, with a total of seven entertainment agencies vying for him to sign with their company. These included JYP, FNC, and Starship Entertainment, which are responsible for debuting famous K-pop groups like Twice, F.T. Island, and Sistar.

Jungkook chose to sign with a smaller company, Big Hit, because he was so impressed with RM, who he saw rapping,

and decided he wanted to train with him.

Jungkook learns by watching and emulating those who inspire him, while developing his own unique style. "The more I watch other artists' performances, the more I want to go on stage. It's an honor to be able to enjoy while receiving inspiration and stimulation," he said in an interview.

Despite his trepidation in the beginning, when he was still navigating life in the spotlight and how to stay grounded, he was sure of one thing: "The *hyungs* really made me." This is what he sings about in hit single, "Begin" on the *Wings* album, where he took the chance to thank his bandmates for helping him find himself at the time when he had no one to depend on.

When I was fifteen years old, I had nothing
The world was too big and I was small
Now I can't even imagine now
I was scentless and completely empty
I pray

Love you my brother, I've got brothers
I discovered emotions, I became me
So I'm me
Now I'm me
. . .
Brother let's cry, cry, cry and get it over with
I don't know much about sadness
But I'm gonna cry anyway
Because, because
You made me again
Fly with me

— **Jungkook, "Begin"**[84]

Now as the stages he performs on get bigger and bigger, Jungkook has found the courage to become more independent. He says he could relate to the character of Sinclair in the book *Demian*, who "wants to break free from the care of others and be an adult, and so do I."

"When I was younger, I thought that everything would just come to me eventually, but now I see I have to take the initiative and practice to improve myself. Before I would do things because I had to, but now I do things on my own," he told *Ize* magazine.

His hard work seems to have been paying off. Unbeknownst to even himself, Jungkook became the "influencer" of the group, who causes products to sell out, even without intending to. Whenever he is seen wearing an item of clothing, drinking or eating a particular brand, or using something

> **"The more I watch other artists' performances, the more I want to go on stage. It's an honor to be able to enjoy while receiving inspiration and stimulation."**
> **—Jungkook**

as random as a fabric softener, the items will become an instant hit among fans—so much so that he became known for having "the Jungkook effect." He doesn't even do it for content marketing or sponsored posts. For instance, ARMYs noticed a book in the background while he was doing a livestream video. They found out it was Kim Soo-hyun's book of essays, *I Decided to Live As Me*, and the book immediately sold out in Korean bookstores and surpassed 600,000 in sales after Jungkook's broadcast.[85]

His selling power and genuine personality have won hearts all over the world, which is probably why a fan account (@bts.jungkook) won the "Instagrammer Global" title at the MTV Millennial Awards—even without having his own Instagram account![86] As of July 2019, Jungkook has also earned the title of "most searched K-pop idol on YouTube."[87]

KIM TAEHYUNG AKA V
Lead Dancer, Vocalist, Visual

A sound of something breaking
I awake from sleep
A sound full of unfamiliarity
Try to cover my ears but can't go to sleep
The pain in my throat gets worse
Try to cover it
I don't have a voice
Today I hear that sound again

. . .

Have I lost myself?
Or have I gained you
I suddenly run to the lake
There's my face in it
                    — V, "Singularity"[88]

IN 2018, INDEPENDENT ARTIST MARC DOMINUS held his first art show in Kettle Art Gallery in Dallas along with other local artists, when, unexpectedly, a group of seven young men casually walked inside to explore the paintings. Dominus wasn't quite familiar with who they were, but something was peculiar as the group was accompanied by security. He was glad otherwise that they were showing interest in his work. "One of the guys said: 'V would like to know if he could have a picture taken with you.' At this point, I still didn't know who he was. Obviously, it was somebody but I didn't know who," Dominus said. The group was BTS, who, at that time were in town to perform a sold-out concert.

The sixty-five-year-old artist had never been featured at an exhibit in a professional setting, much less have his work bought by someone he didn't know personally. He often trades his paintings or sells them to "friends or friends of friends." And just when he thought he would continue living a peaceful life pursuing his art as he always did, several BTS fans would come up and have their picture taken with him. He recalls, "That night, not only did I sell a painting to a complete stranger, I sold two paintings to a complete stranger. An extraordinarily famous stranger."[89]

His paintings are bright, colorful, and lighthearted, yet evoke a mysterious air about them, and it was BTS's V who went home with two of them that rainy night.

school days, he took saxophone lessons and dreamed of becoming a professional saxophonist, and eventually wanted to become a singer. "It's just my imagination but I want to sing on stage alongside a trumpeter or pianist. I really like lyrical music, so I hope instead of an exciting song, my song can be [kind of] healing to people."

V (which stands for "Victory"), whose real name is Kim Taehyung, has always been interested in the field of art. "I became a fan of Van Gogh after I fell in love at first sight with the piece 'Starry Night.' I have six paintings hanging up at my home. Recently I've started gaining interest in other painters as well, like Roy Lichtenstein, Gustav Klimt, Marc Chagall, and Claude Monet," he explained in a feature with a Japanese magazine.

V graduated from Korean Arts High School, and his passion for music and art was always there as a child. In his elementary

> **I've spent most of my life as BTS's V. On one hand I'm happy that 'V's' existence grew much bigger than what I was dreaming of, but there are also times that I want to live as Kim Taehyung . . . This is just an 'if' but even if the cheers become smaller in the future, as long as ARMYs' voices exist, our happiness will continue on."**
>
> **—V**

At that time, taking up a career in the arts was not a practical move for him as a young man who had come from humble beginnings in his hometown of Daegu. He grew up in a family of farmers, yet his parents would always encourage him in his creative interests.

"I came from a poor family and I never thought I would become famous," V revealed in an interview. "[Being a star] is a lucky chance that I can only come across once in a lifetime. If I wasn't in BTS I would probably become a farmer. I'd be pulling out weeds from a farm with my grandmother."

When Big Hit Entertainment held a talent search in Daegu, it was by sheer accident that V would come across the opportunity to audition, and with his unique charm, he became the only person to pass. He had gone along to support a friend, but one of the staff saw potential in V and encouraged him to try out on the spot.

Despite how far he's come, he has never forgotten about his roots and often longs for the warmth of his family and simple life back home.

"I've spent most of my life as BTS's V. On one hand I'm happy that 'V's' existence grew much bigger than what I was dreaming of, but there are also times that I want to live as Kim Taehyung," he shared in the *BTS Wings Concept Book*. "Like, eating delicious

Korean food with family. But the cheers that the ARMYs send us with a smile are our happiness right now. I'm able to relax during concerts, since I'm making memories with them who are like family to me. This moment, right here, is my utmost moment of youth! This is just an 'if' but even if the cheers become smaller in the future, as long as ARMYs' voices exist, our happiness will continue on."[90]

I'll sacrifice myself to protect you
I'll do it obviously
I will make this crisis into an opportunity
You are my best decision, nothing can stop me
Take me into the scattered light
To the end of the world
— **V's verse in "It's Definitely You"**[91]

As for his role in BTS, V is known for his deep, soulful vocals combined with a wide vocal range. An article in *Billboard* raved about his "deep tone and expressive vocals that are a mainstay to BTS's sound."[92] He has released solo singles on some of the group's albums, namely, "4 O'Clock" featuring RM, "Stigma," and "Winter Bear," the first solo all-English ballad from a BTS member.

He says he aspires "to become a singer who can make ARMYs proud. A singer whose fans can go anywhere saying, my idol is BTS and people around would marvel, 'Wow.'"

When the cameras are on, V has shown his other talent: his acting chops, which have enabled him to make his Korean drama debut in *Hwarang*, alongside other well-

known actors in Korea. In between shooting days, he would still perform onstage with BTS, not wanting to disappoint the other BTS members and fans. "There certainly were stressful times, but I couldn't use the excuse of having to film a drama to show I'm tired when the other members were also working hard on the tour," he said in the *BTS Wings Concept Book*.

But when the cameras are off, V possesses an exuberant, off-beat personality that many fans would fondly call his "duality." Despite his cool, stylish exterior—he is also known as the fashionista of the group—V is often playful and blurts out quirky humor that lightens up the band's mood. It also reflects his outlook in life: "Actually, I don't quite like it when everything's set in place, so I get more nervous if it's scripted or planned out . . . Just go with it, this was my mindset."

Despite all praises, V maintains a humble heart. "I'm sensitive about my performance. I think the members are the same, too. We have to judge our performances with a cool head. We change our expressions and gestures every stage but there's always a lot of regrets left. What should I do to fully dominate the stage? I'm curious."[93]

PARK JIMIN AKA JIMIN
Main Dancer, Lead Vocalist

All this is no coincidence
Just, just, by my feeling
The whole world is different from yesterday
Just, just, with your joy

When you called me
I became your flower
As if we were waiting
We bloom until we ache

Maybe it's the providence of the universe
It just had to be that
You know, I know
You are me, I am you
                    — **Jimin, "Serendipity"**[94]

WHEN HE MOVES, IT'S AS IF THE WHOLE WORLD spins with him. He glides on the dance floor like a delicate swan, yet his every movement and facial expression tell a story of anguish, passion, love, sensuality, and hope. This is Jimin, whose background in contemporary dance adds a touch of drama and casts a captivating spell in all of BTS's performances.

Having grown up attending a dance academy in Busan and being trained in modern dance, Jimin's work ethos echoes that of a novice dancer who grows into perfection through a lifetime of dedicated practice.

"I cut down on sleep a lot. I woke up early before going to school to practice, during lunch time, after school and continued again until dawn. I only take a short nap and start dancing again. This repeated for about a year," he recalled.[95] "I wasn't making any progress in dancing or singing. So I worked even harder . . . No matter how far I think

> **"If our songs, concerts and existence become the reason why someone is able to face forward, I want to continue running, and I think we will."**
> **—JIMIN**

I have gotten, when looking back, I'm still at the same place. This tired me out a lot before."

Even after passing the auditions, being added as the last member to join BTS, and eventually breaking into superstardom, Jimin still maintains his disciplined mindset with each stage, like a professional dancer who is always training for the best performance of his life. He always puts his best foot forward, even after the curtain falls. "Doing my best with the thought of having nothing to offer except for my performance, I think it's important to not lose that thought."

Jimin's graceful movements and handsome features caught the attention of many creative artists all over the world, with him emerging as a muse for works of art in Korea, France, and England. Artists would use different media to incorporate his image in their creations. Artist Lee.K wrote an explanation of a work featuring Jimin on canvas: "My intention was to showcase the colors of K-pop and how much it revolves around me on a personal level. I have chosen Jimin to represent the K-pop genre and to let the audience see the level of influence as well as growth that K-pop has, not only on me but also on a worldwide scale. However, to ensure that the idea doesn't come across as an obsession, I have associated Jimin in my childhood memories of a theme park."[96]

I'm still standing here with my eyes closed
Lost between the deserts and oceans
I'm still wandering
Where should I go yeah
I didn't know there were this many
Paths I can't go and paths I can't take
I never felt this way before
Am I becoming an adult?

. . .

Lost my way
Constantly pushing without rest
Within the harsh rainstorms
Lost my way
Within a complicated world without an exit
Lost my way
Lost my way
No matter how much I wander
I want to believe in my path
— Jimin's verse in "Lost"[97]

Despite being one of the younger members of BTS, Jimin shows maturity in his thinking. When asked about their colossal success, he said, "If our songs, concerts and existence become the reason why someone is able to face forward, I want to continue running, and I think we will. When we started the UNICEF project last year, RM said something like this: 'I don't know how many people we're going to be able to inspire. But if even one person can become inspired, there's meaning in us doing it.' These words influenced me a lot."[98]

He has released two solo tracks, "Lie" and "Serendipity," which surpassed 50 million streams on Spotify in 2019, breaking the record held by Psy's "Gentleman," a catchy track that went viral worldwide in 2013. Jimin's co-written song "Promise" also

claimed a top spot in Soundcloud as the biggest 24-hour debut ever.[99] *Billboard* is all praise for the modern dancer, saying he "took things to another level with his expressive delivery of the song's dramatic choreography, telling a message as much with his body as his vocals."

Off-camera with the other members, Jimin shows a softer side to himself, one that is quite opposite from his strong charisma onstage. In an interview with *Exile* magazine, J-Hope was translated as saying, "Jimin is very cute. He's always so cute. He's the kind of person born with a natural cuteness. And even though he's younger than me, he sometimes acts like a dependable older brother, which is another charming side of him."[100]

CHAPTER 8

THE OTHER SIDE OF THE STORY: A ROUGH ROAD TO THE TOP

RESISTANCE, DOUBT, STRUGGLE, AND PREJUDICE often find those that are new in the mainstream. This seems to have been the case for BTS at the time of their debut until they reached number one. Their success story is far from instant as it was fraught with hardships, controversies, and naysayers along the way.

BTS members have been pretty vocal about their trepidations through their songs and interviews. Similar to the dilemma of idols who have trained for years under an agency, their biggest concerns were: "When will they ever debut?" And if they do, will they "make it"?

When they were still training, the members of BTS often had self-doubts and worries aside from the pressures they feel from the rigid schedules of singing, dancing, language, acting, hosting, and many other lessons they needed to take for them to be able to thrive in the competitive entertainment scene. They were, after all, plucked from their homes and isolated far from their friends and families for a long period of time. That must have felt endless for them. Their dreams of being in the spotlight definitely came with a price.

For BTS, their passion for music was all they had to console their uncertainties, and their friendship provided them comfort to get through another day. This was made clear by the band in their hidden track, "Skit: On the Start Line," a skit off their *2 Cool 4 Skool* album:

Trainee
In many ways, this term defines my existence
But at the same time it is a term that I can
    never truly explain
A period of time, a state of transition
Where I could neither belong anywhere
Nor do anything
. . .
Though I came here through a certain
    confidence
And belief in myself
What awaited me was a different kind of
    reality:
Even now, after three years have passed
Even as I occasionally gain the self-
    certainty to think things like
"once I debut, I will conquer the music industry"
Whenever I hear the criticisms of the
    producers and teachers
I am again overwhelmed by the realization
    that I am nothing
That I am as inconsequential as a speck of
    dust
It's as if though before me lies the bluest
    ocean
And if I turn to look back
A vast desert awaits me
    — **BTS, "Skit: On the Start Line"**[101]

The track was their heartfelt confession as they prepared themselves for debut, finally "graduating" from their trainee years to become future stars. Suga once said in an interview that there was a time when they didn't have enough time to eat or sleep—while RM reminisced about how he never made other friends aside from his school classmates and he would feel sad when he would hear about them moving on with their lives while he continued to practice in the studio.

Even though they expressed how difficult it was for them and how, at some point, their confidence levels dipped to all-time lows, they still considered their trainee years as sort of an honor badge or a rite of passage they had to overcome to reach their destination. As RM's rough voice sang in the track, "Even after I debut, new oceans and new deserts will likely await me. I am not afraid because it has made me who I am."

When BTS debuted with their song "No More Dream" in 2013, Big Hit Entertainment was a small company with little budget for promotions, but they had big goals: to launch the band as a talented, fearless, straightforward group who wanted to shatter long-established conventions in K-pop and society in general. The song received a tepid response, with their next single "We Are Bulletproof Pt. 2" failing to reach "major hit" categories. They did not make a big splash like they had originally planned.

To be clear, BTS was not the first band to compose their own songs and challenge the "idol" image. One close example, among many others, is Seo Taiji and Boys, a trio from the early '90s that sparked ideas about counterculture and sang political songs that challenged censorship standards of that extremely conservative time in Korea. Another influential group is Big Bang—a five-member group from YG Entertainment with almost fifteen years of experience and international success—who have released songs that spoke to the youth, with groundbreaking musical styles that were imaginative and creative. Big Bang was the coolest, a trendsetting group that had an aspirational image: designer wardrobes, expensive cars and jewelry, out-of-this-world parties, and the like.

BTS's approach was quite different. They came from the gritty side of hip-hop, their songs and music videos not glossed with flashy, gimmicky themes that were often expected of rookies. They sang about breaking free from peer pressure, addressing youth issues, and encouraging listeners to find their own voice. So why didn't they appeal to audiences when they first came onto the scene?

BTS's rough start was due to different factors. Not only was the market not ready for experimental styles, Big Hit was also not in the same league as the other "big three" agencies at that time. Their broadcast appearances were made relatively shorter by TV stations in favor of more popular groups, lessening their chances for exposure.

Moreover, their old-school hip-hop sound and fierce imagery were deemed outdated and "too much" or "too strong" by both critics and audiences in South Korea who were used to the impeccably polished songs from near perfect-looking K-pop idols. Other critics claimed that the delinquent or rebellious nature of BTS was a contrived concept that merely aimed to seek attention rather than share an underlying message.

"We failed and tried again, and failed and tried again," Suga said in a discussion with the BBC. "I think people saw that process and gained a lot of encouragement from it." RM shared the same outlook, "Every good thing require[s] the struggles."

They started achieving moderate success when they released *Skool Luv Affair*, which topped the Gaon Music Chart, with the lead single "Boy in Luv" having the same hard rock, old-school hip-hop vibes but with a catchier sound. BTS's performance in the charts would also improve over the next couple of years, with albums *Dark and Wild* and *The Most Beautiful Moment in Life Pt. 1* gaining traction and peaking in rankings and sales records in Korea.

But BTS would again encounter huge hurdles, this time among "fandoms," large numbers of fan communities that focused on supporting more established groups. Several fandoms banded together and made accusations against the band, making 2016 a year when BTS had a lot of "anti-fans."

The anti-fans found ways to discredit BTS with groundless allegations, from plagiarizing another group's photo shoot concept and Big Hit buying their own artists' albums to boost sales,[102] to something as inconsequential as copying an idol's style of clothing or hair color.

This wasn't a simple and petty squabble among a group of fans. The anti-fans further staged efforts to deter BTS's own fanbase from growing and disrupted their promotions and concerts. A detailed "Twitter attack" was planned by anti's, aimed at one of BTS's concerts in Seoul Olympic Park. The notice instructed anti-fans to post and retweet the hashtags #plagiarismboyscouts or #bangtanplagiarism once the concert began until thirty minutes after it ended. "Let's show them all of the fandoms' combined forces, let's show those cancerous girls"—the Korean word for cancer phonetically sounds similar to the beginning of ARMY—"our combined forces. Just upload any hashtags and words related to Bangtan's copying/plagiarizing controversies."[103]

RM, who has also received extreme backlash for his expletive-filled song, "Joke," acknowledged that they are still prone to making errors and learning from their mistakes. "Not just our members but our producers are talking about social issues, meeting with experts and reading a lot of books. We still have a long way to go, but we'll think hard, take in criticism and mature," he said at a press conference. He

BTS receives recognition at the 2018 Korean Popular Culture And Arts Awards at Olympic Hall on October 24, 2018 in Seoul.

BTS expresses shock and joy upon winning the Top Duo/Group trophy during the 2019 Billboard Music Awards.

also assured the audience that all of them do their homework by "discuss[ing] the problems together with experts from each field," proving critics who labeled them as just another typical boy band wrong.

BTS may have had their own share of missteps and unfortunate moments, but the worst attack toward them was extreme: anonymous online death threats directed at members of the band. In 2018, *Billboard* reported on a post from a user that revealed disturbing details about their intent to shoot Jimin during his solo performance at BTS's concert in Fort Worth, Texas.[104]

Authorities were notified and investigated the matter, with Big Hit issuing a statement that they would take "necessary measures against activities that threaten the safety of its members and fans."

An odd kid
He sang as if he was breathing
Wherever was fine
He only wanted to do music
Only singing
The thing that made his heart beat
Although he walked down the only path

It's not easy
Failure and frustration
Words that someone gave me after calling
    me, exhausted, to stop

You're a singing star
You're a singing star
But I see no star . . .
After some years passed by

. . .

I got fed up by you cutely bragging about
   your money on TV
My passport is about to die from overworking
You're the ones who benefitted from
   media, hahahaha
Hey, hey, you're the ones who're better at
   playing celebrities
We're still the same as back then
                — BTS, "Airplane Pt. 2[105]

Aside from anti-fan attacks, BTS also encountered another challenge: proving their legitimacy and authenticity as rappers, particularly RM and Suga. Among many self-made singer-songwriters and professionals in the Korean music industry, the term "idol" is often looked down upon as merely an entertainer who is simply "not a true artist." With BTS falling into this category, detractors sought to dampen the group's public perception. Korean rapper B-Free did this when he criticized the group's makeup and dancing, saying "they look like girls."[106]

After negative reactions from ARMYs, the rapper attempted to lighten his remarks by posting on Twitter in English, "Truly bless (sic) to have come from nothing and have people talking about me. Only makes me want to work harder and make better music and maybe I can be a better person in the

process. I just make fun of things from a perspective where if a man wears makeup and dance like Lady Gaga, I just meant to make fun and that's it."

The rapper showed no signs of stopping, as he cursed ARMYs and called Suga and RM "people who could have continued on the path to become rappers but couldn't resist the temptation of money." He also questioned the band's music category, asking, "Is BTS's music hip hop?" and "Is wearing makeup like a girl on stage hip hop?"[107] He claimed that both rappers did not deserve to be called as such because they became "sell-outs" as idols.

That was in 2013, and perhaps after years of reflection or most likely from having difficulties promoting after the incident (his videos were bombarded with hateful comments and downvotes/dislikes), B-Free changed his tone and issued an official apology in July 2019, addressed to BTS and their fans, asking forgiveness for the "emotional pain he's caused."

Fans have called his statement "too late" and "insincere," pointing out the questionable timing of his apology when BTS had already become worldwide stars.

The members of BTS stayed silent and refrained from addressing the issues through interviews, but instead expressed their feelings through one way they know best: their lyrics. Suga wrote a fiery rap song included in his solo mixtape about people trying to bring others down, while he equated success to hard work.

If you're going to leave
Take back whatever you've said before
If you ask me how I've succeeded
I don't really have an answer
But at least, I slept less and stayed active
Compared to you all to grow up

I'm still not sure about the secret to success
But I think I know the secret to failure
The secret is to play the fool just like you
And keep blabbing your mouth
But I wouldn't live like that even if I had to die
. . .
I don't care if you keep
Digging your own grave or wasting yourself
So please continue living like that
— **Agust D (Suga), "Give It to Me"**[108]

In the waiting room and between performances
I hold a pen and write the lyrics
This is how I am, did something about me
    change before your eyes?
Damn, shit I'm still the same
I changed, you say? (what?) Go and tell them
. . .
And let the haters hate on me
 It's a day job they've always been at
While you were teasing the keyboard I
    fulfilled my dreams
Sunglasses, hairstyle, I know why you
    ridicule me
In any case, it's me who's gone further than
    you at age 20
. . .

BTS at the 2019 Seoul Music Awards where they won Best Album and Daesang, the biggest recognition for the year.

BTS backstage after winning Top Social Artist Award at the 2018 BBMAs.

I'm a born singer A little belated confession
   (I swear)
The mirage that always seemed so far
   away is now before my eyes (It's here)
I'm a born singer perhaps an early confession
But I'm so happy I'm good
                    — BTS, "Born Singer"[109]

While they may not have yet achieved massive commercial success a year or two after debuting in their home country, things were different abroad. With BTS's social media and promotional content made highly accessible online, the international audiences started taking notice of the band, noting that they had a unique sound and a different perspective. Their biggest international break came with the release of their *Wings* EP and subsequent megahit songs like "DNA," "Mic Drop," "Fake Love," and "Idol." Their songs seamlessly combined high-energy hip-hop, dance, EDM, and genre-fluid music that a lot of non-Korean-speaking listeners enjoyed.

But more than their music, what brought fans closer to them was their rags-to-riches story, or more specifically, their journey from being idols to icons. They have shown that there is truth to the age-old adage: "With persistence and passion, anyone can achieve their dreams," Lee Jee-heng, a culture researcher who released the book *BTS and ARMY Culture* explained. "Among K-pop singers, [they] began from the lowest place, and that is why fans cheer for their efforts in overcoming limits."[110]

"We didn't realize we were becoming famous until we were invited to KCONs [K-pop music festivals] in the U.S. and Europe in 2014 or 2015," RM shared in an interview. "Thousands of fans were calling our name at the venue, and almost everyone memorized the Korean lyrics of our songs, which was amazing and overwhelming. Who would have thought that people from across the ocean, Europe, the U.S., South America, even Tahiti, would love our songs and performances, just by watching them on YouTube? We were just grateful . . . and we still are."

BTS would still be hounded by issues even later on after they achieved international fame, with Bang Si-hyuk expressing in his commencement speech his firm stance against malicious criticisms against BTS: "Our artists, who are enjoying global reputation and give comfort and move fans, are hurt by groundless criticism by anonymous people. There are still so many cases where contents, the product of our blood, sweat, and tears are unfairly distributed and used as a means of filling pockets of unethical people. That's why I am always angry, and has (sic) been fighting against these problems. It's still continuing."

CHAPTER 9

THE WORDS AND SOUNDS OF THEIR DREAMS: UNDERSTANDING BTS SONGS AND MUSIC VIDEOS

Songs convey what the heart cannot express through mere words alone. The coalescence of each note, melody, sound, as told through every choreographed movement and amplified by lights, costumes, and strong imagery, among many other things, make up a fulfilled whole of one single BTS song. Their songs carry the weight of yearning, anxiety, fear, and frustration, while celebrating the lightness of youth, love, gratitude, and ultimately, the self.

There is something intriguing about BTS's lyrics that are a collaborative product of seven people in their early twenties, who all write with such maturity and universality that hit the nerves of listeners from all walks of life. Their strong, exciting songs have an otherworldly depth and mission: to call out injustice, to awaken, inform, and warn. Their ballads evoke a feeling of "*Han*," which, according to a review by *Variety* writer Kim Jae Ha, means a "wistful combination of longing and sorrow."[111]

"This adult 'Han' element also explains why Bangtan's fandom cohort is unusually diverse for a K-pop artist. Although Korean history is uniquely saturated in themes of melancholy, struggle and hope, they are ultimately ageless, universal concepts. Therefore, unlike other K-pop fandoms, BTS fans span every age, gender and ethnic group—BTS is not a 'crazy' teenage phenomenon, it is an intellectual phenomenon," writes Sarah C for *Medium*.[112]

Whether in regular verse, chorus, or rap section, their words play within flights of poetry, many of which RM, wanting to be a poet himself, penned. "In a time where the melody and good vibes are important, as someone who wanted to become a poet, as I wanted to become a writer, the audible feel of the words and the beauty of the lyrics are more important," he explained during a V Live session where he detailed his process on *Map of the Soul: Persona*.[113]

He also said he was able to come up with "the best and most beautiful words" for the people he is grateful to, "those who have made me where I am now."

"We had to super focus and pick really carefully. We had to choose the right rough gem," he added. J-Hope jumps in: "I think we all try hard to do our roles whether it's writing lyrics or songs. We try to participate together as much as we can. And our participation in the process makes the music more sincere, and then changes our attitude of how we approach ourselves."

Their creative process does not only involve the emotional and intellectual part of songwriting, it also entails being hands-on with the technical aspects that make up the song. "Each artist has their own preferences and pace, and each sound engineer has their own sphere of artistry," Suga, a producer himself, said at the Grammy U event. "Every venue is different, so we sit down and meet with engineers and make sure we communicate. The most important thing is to be sensitive."

Their themes are cohesive and all-encompassing with their videos that are threaded together by metaphors, symbolism, and references from literature, films, and social reality—and all of these elements make the viewers think. When watching a BTS music video, one doesn't necessarily need to do so chronologically in the order of their release. At times, fans discover that BTS's videos make more sense when they are put into context with their other videos and trailers.

The band's vision is actualized with the help of their creative staff of graphic artists, stylists, filmmakers, scriptwriters, and the production team, Lumpens, which have worked on most of their videos. Lumpens is a filmmaking company known for their well-thought-out storylines and signature stylish cinematic works.

"BTS members are given the chance to give input to the visual elements and storytelling once the basic concept is set up," one of the staff members told *Billboard*. "The storytelling as a whole is designed to represent each member in terms of reality, as well as in a fictional narrative. It's better to involve everyone as much as we can, and that's how we continue to have a very strong narrative throughout the series of albums."[114]

Singer Halsey—who was featured on the song "Boy with Luv" and is a close friend of BTS's members—said during a radio interview that she got inspired by the creativity and ingenuity of their videos. "I was watching some of their earlier videos and I saw some of them had philosophical references and the way they use colors and the warmness . . . Just all of it is so layered."

The audiences also became part of the greater conversation of their music, videos, and performances, where BTS opened the doors to fan interpretations and "fan theories." It's a communal activity done in online spaces where there can be no right or wrong answers in discussions, just a shared passion for the band and the puzzles they put out for fans online. In that sense, BTS bridges distances in languages and cultural differences, as their messages come through the pieces that the fans eventually put together.

"We started to tell the stories that people wanted to hear and were ready to hear, stories that other people could not or would not tell," Suga shared. "We said what other people were feeling—like pain, anxieties and worries."

Here, we explore the overarching themes and meanings behind some of their most iconic songs and music videos.

"NO MORE DREAM"

Riding in a big, yellow school bus with one member at the steering wheel, BTS seemed to have escaped from a day in school. The bus hit a couple of boxes stacked up on an abandoned street, before the group left the bus to sing and dance, all while angrily destroying everything in their sight. They were also seen throwing away papers and books in the backdrop of a blackboard filled with written equations and formulas.

They started the song by asking, "Hey, what's your dream?"

I wanna big house, big cars & big rings
But in reality, I don't have any big dreams
Haha I live an easy life
Even if I don't dream, no one says anything
    to me
Everyone is thinking the same as me
When we were still young
I said I'll go to some university
Okay, mum, I'm going to the library
. . .
Boring same day, every day repeats
Adults and parents tell us the same dream
Future job number one, public officials?
It's not a forced dream, a relief pitcher
                    — BTS, "No More Dream"[115]

BTS's first release from their album *2 Cool 4 Skool*, "No More Dream," which was the first single off their three-part school trilogy, set the tone for their upcoming releases both in imagery and theme. The band alluded to the strict standards set by adults for impressionable youths: study hard, enter a prestigious university, get a good job, earn money, and become an obedient member of society. Anyone who deviates from this order was bound for failure. This song portrays the endless pattern that has been passed down from generation to generation, with the youth turning into voiceless robots that follow the no-fail "formula for success" defined by those who preceded them. Jungkook explained in an interview, "Living without passion is like being dead." V reinforced the thought when he was quoted to have said, "Don't be trapped in someone else's dream."[116]

"College is presented like some sort of cure-all," Suga explained. "They say that if you go, your life will be set. But this isn't the reality, and they realize that was all a lie. No one else can take responsibility for you at that point."

"No More Dream" calls for the youth to wake up from this vicious cycle, urging them to find their real passion and happiness, instead of the "forced dreams" parents and other adults imposed on them. It's no wonder BTS seemed to literally shatter things around them in the video: it was a form of rebellion, a cry to break free from "the ways Korean kids feel stymied by societal expectations," as *Time* puts it, while *Billboard* interpreted it as a commentary on "how kids are forced to give up their dreams in order to appease their parents."

This theme would later appear again in their song, "Baepsae," which discusses the generational gap experienced by today's youth. "Our generation has had it hard," RM raps. "Thanks to those that came before us I'm spread too thin. Change the rules, but the ones who came before us want to maintain."

The last verses of "No More Dream" represent the band's final act of defiance as they tell the adults: "It's all a lie. Why are you telling me to go another way? Do well for yourself! Don't push others!"

"N.O"

WITH THEIR BLANK, COLD STARES AND
expressionless faces, BTS, wearing military-
esque uniforms, moved their heads left,
right, and down as they were told. They were
seated inside a futuristic, spotless classroom,
surrounded by military guards dressed all
in white. The leader, holding a truncheon,
instructed the guards to give them red pills to
swallow, after which mathematical formulas
and equations in bold, red colors appeared
on their desks. One by one, the members
clenched their fists, as indignation built up
amongst them. They all stood up and pushed
against the defensive shields of the armed
guards until they were able to crack open
the walls of the room. When they emerged,
the BTS members were all wearing white,
descending down a flight of stairs as the
song reached its climax.

A good house, a good car, will these things
    bring happiness?
In Seoul to the SKY, would your parents be
    happy?
Dream is gone, no time to breathe
School, house and PC room is all we have
We live the same life
And have to become number one
For us it's like a double spy between dream
    and reality
Who is the one who made us into study
    machines?
It's either number one or a failure
They trap us in borders, the adults
There's no choice but to consent

Even if we think simply, it's the survival of
    the fittest
Who do you think is the one who makes us
    step on even our close friends to climb
    up? What?
Everybody say NO!
It can't be any later
Don't be trapped in someone else's dream
We roll (We roll) We roll (We roll) We roll
                                    — BTS, "N.O"[117]

The song and music video for "N.O"
picked up where "No More Dream" left off,
this time with more impactful visuals and
bolder choreography that aimed to make
a big statement. Highly symbolic of law
enforcement or authoritarian control, the
dystopian world of white-uniformed guards
versus the group wearing black was created
to show the disparate views between adults
and young people.

To understand this recurring theme
throughout BTS's initial song releases, it
is important to know where their anger is
coming from. To put this in context, South
Korean society puts a huge emphasis on
educational achievement and compliance,
a deeply ingrained mindset that has been
embedded in Korean culture for decades. A
normal student might spend grueling hours
all day in school studying math, English, and
other subjects until 11 p.m. Once they get
back home, they might again be forced by
their parents to review their studies to get
perfect test scores, leaving them with no time
to rest or hang out with friends. Many do this

every day to get ahead of the competition, to rank at top of the class, and be accepted at any one of Korea's most elite universities. NPR writer Elise Hu referred to it in her article as the "all-work, no-play culture of South Korean education."

"It's not about finding your own path or your own self as it is about doing better than those around you. It's in many ways a zero sum game for South Korean students," says Tom Owenby, an English and AP History teacher in Seoul. Meanwhile, Kim Mee Suk, a researcher at the Korea Institute for Health and Social Affairs, which studied the stress levels of Korean students, said, "It's kind of alarming, actually. If young students [are] not happy, we cannot guarantee their happiness when they grow up, so our future will be really dark . . . We don't have enough natural resources; the only resources we have [are] human resources. So actually everybody equipped with higher education would be best for our country but not good for their own selves. So we have a really big dilemma."[118] The study concluded that Koreans as young as eleven to fifteen years of age experience high levels of stress, with the pressure to excel taking its toll on their mental health.

What BTS was singing was not about abandoning responsibilities, per se. As one of the most memorable lines in "N.O" says, "Outside, there are so many kids like me, living the life of a puppet. Who will take responsibility?"

Instead, BTS was telling the youth to also take responsibility for themselves and not just blindly follow what they are told to do. They wanted their listeners to ask the fundamental questions, "Why?" "What is my purpose?" "What is my dream?"

"I NEED U" and "RUN"

WHILE BTS IS MOSTLY KNOWN FOR THEIR powerful songs, they show their vulnerable side through ballads that bare their souls. "I Need U" is the song that probably proved to the whole world that the group has what it takes to switch effortlessly from hip-hop to more soulful, slower songs. It was a shift to a romantic theme, which not only explored the joy of love, but also the pain, isolation, heartbreak, and longing that come along with it.

You can't do this to me
All of the things you said are like a mask
It hides the truth and rips me apart
It pierces me, I'm going crazy, I hate this
Take it all away, I hate you

. . .

I'm sorry (I hate you)
I love you (I hate you)
Forgive me

It goes round and round, why do I keep
    coming back
I go down and down, at this point, I'm just
    a fool
Whatever I do, I can't help it
It's definitely my heart, my feelings but why
    don't they listen to me
. . .
I need you girl, you're beautiful
I need you girl, you're so cold
                    — BTS, "I Need U"[119]

In the "I Need U" video, the members were shown during different moments of misery.

Each have their own backstory that was not fully revealed, leaving the audience wondering how they ended up in their dire situations. The same melancholic vibe is portrayed in "Run," where scenes go back and forth between reality and dream states, as seen in each of the member's flashbacks. In one scene a member is shown confronting a group of violent thugs in a dark alley, another one is trapped in a hospital, while two members get caught by the authorities. In the next scene they were shown partying, laughing, and having fun as if nothing happened. Is it the past or present? Which world is real?

Everything seemed pretty ambivalent and mysterious, with hidden clues planted in each scene. What was made clear, however, was that they all get together in the end, receiving comfort in each other's company as they run and escape from their dark lives while looking toward the sea.

I run, run, run
I can't stop
Run, run, run again
I can't help it
This is all I can do anyway
All I know is how to love you

Run, run, run again
It's okay to fall
Run, run. Run, again
It's okay to get hurt
I'm alright, even if I can't have you
Pitiful destiny, point your finger at me
                    — BTS, "Run"[120]

To understand each of their narratives, one must look into the series of Webtoons produced by Big Hit Entertainment. One such Webtoon is titled "Save Me," and is made up of fifteen episodes. The summary goes: "Seven boys. Best friends. Their fates intertwined through the good times together, but also the tough times, as they have gone their separate ways and suffered greatly as a result. When all is almost lost for these boys, one is given a special chance to go back in time and help his friends fix the mistakes that led them down this path. He'll do anything to save them, but can he? Or is he too late?"[121]

Some of their earlier and later videos were actually connected to the "Bangtan Universe," an overarching plotline that is inspired by each member of BTS, and explains the meaning behind their teasers, skits, and music videos. This recurring "universe" appeared in the Hwayang Yonghwa Trilogy (HHYH, aka "The Most Beautiful Moment in Life"), with videos like "I Need U," "Run," "Prologue," "Fire," and "Young Forever," tackling the main theme, which is "youth."

The Bangtan Theory website interprets the HYYH Trilogy as "simply a coming of age story. It tells the struggles the boys are facing while transitioning from childhood to adulthood, from being caterpillars to becoming butterflies (chrysalis stage)."[122]

Again, when watching BTS videos, it is important to remember that most of them are connected, and each scene is shown in a different order. So viewers need to piece them together one by one. Deciphering music videos has become such a huge part of the fandom that several websites and forums have been created so that fans can discuss their own takes on the enigmatic videos.

The series has been produced into short films, web toons, books, and videos all centered around BTS. It is this kind of creativity and unique storytelling that made their songs more compelling, with the content made into different forms of media.

Not a lot of K-pop artists have done this kind of "concept within a concept" production when it comes to making music videos, as BTS has done so consistently. The group doesn't always follow trends, but instead they keep true to their goal of making content that has a lot of meanings. This is why fans can't get enough and it makes the hunt for hints so much more exciting.

"DOPE"

I reject rejection
I'm always over the top
Dope, dope, dope, dope
I Reject rejection
You all work for me
Dope, dope, dope

Given up on 3? Given up on 5?
I like the number 6, how about giving up on 6?
The media and adults say we don't have
   the willpower, condemning us like stocks
Why are they killing us before we can even
   try, enemy enemy enemy
Why are you hanging your head and
   accepting it already? energy energy energy
Don't ever give up, you know you not lonely
Our dawn is prettier than the day
So can I get a little bit of hope yeah
Wake your sleeping youth, go
                    — BTS, "Dope"[123]

To THOSE THAT ONLY KNOW SOUTH KOREA through K-dramas and K-pop, it may seem like an exciting, dreamy place to live, a country with stylish citizens, great food, and the perfect harmony between beautiful, historic landmarks and modern, Instagrammable skylines. Even though it is true that South Korea has long risen as one of the world's most innovative, economically developed, and dynamic first world countries, there are numerous issues that reveal the decay that is hidden beneath its bright, inviting facade.

BTS shines light on these issues, which are often left to be discussed in news broadcasts and online forums. One of the songs that calls for the youth to join the discussion is "Dope," an upbeat dance song with a catchy hook and intense saxophone sounds. It starts off as song with a lot of "swag," with lines such as "I'm different from the other guys," and "I'm kinda awesome." This is the surface meaning of the slang "dope," after all, which refers to an unapologetic sense of confidence for being or having done something great. But as the song progresses, one will realize that it is talking about a more serious topic: the situation of youth unemployment and disillusionment in Korea.

The country's current president, Moon Jae-in, called this issue a potential "national disaster," and if it continues the young citizens could turn into a "lost generation."[124] The *Financial Times* reported that as of February 2019, South Korea unemployment rose to a nine-year high, at around 4.4 percent.[125]

In previous songs, BTS rallied against the strict disciplinarian culture of Korean education and the society, which frowns upon people who "follow their dreams." Here, the group digs in deeper and highlights the fact that the country's extremely competitive market, impossibly high standards, and harsh hierarchical work culture prevent young people from finding fulfilling jobs. Ironically, Koreans are overeducated but under- and unemployed. Accompanied by declining job opportunities and inflation, student loans and debts are getting higher, leaving the current and previous generations with no choice but to give up on important things such as marriage, family, childbirth, interpersonal relationships, home ownership—and ultimately, happiness.

The lyrics referring to this are "sam," "oh," and "yook," which are the Korean numbers three, five, and six. More specifically, these are the "Sampo," "Ohpo," and "Yookpo" generations, with each sacrificing different things in order to survive. This is a popular expression in Korea, where the "Sampo" generation gave up their desires for relationships and marriage, the "Ohpo" gave up employment and stability, while the youngest among these generations, "Yookpo," gave up on all aspects. But even if these sacrifices were done out of necessity,

society looks down on them as millennials who simply have given up. RM's rap goes, "Why are you killing us before we can try?"

To drive this point even further, the group was wearing different uniforms of professions that are considered good jobs: doctor, company worker, police officer, and others.

"Honestly, from our standpoint, every day is stressful for our generation. It's hard to get a job, it's harder to attend college now more than ever," RM told *Billboard*.[126] "Adults need to create policies that can facilitate that overall social change. Right now, the privileged class, the upper class needs to change the way they think." Suga continues, "And this isn't just Korea, but the rest of the world. The reason why our music resonates with people around the world who are in their teens, 20s and 30s is because of these issues."

"GO GO"

At first listen, the song "Go Go" sounds like a cool anthem for a tropical beach party or a reckless night out with friends. The word *YOLO*, which is the abbreviated form of "you only live once," keeps repeating in the track, almost like an entrancing mantra inviting anyone craving mindless adventure.

The song was not accompanied by an official music video, but BTS performed it live on Korean music programs. The choreography featured catchy movements to exciting beats, with the boys wearing colorful hoodies and sportswear while making animated facial expressions. But Suga urged everyone to listen to the song again: "It isn't a BTS album if there isn't a track criticizing society."

"Go Go" does, in fact, poke fun at people's illusions of grandeur and impractical tendency to live beyond their means. "The current generation uses phrases like YOLO and having fun squandering money, but I don't think people think about why they use such terms so much even while using [them]," Suga added.[127]

Dollar dollar
Squandering it all in one day
Run, run, I make and waste my own money
Run, run, run, run
Run, run

I want to be cruisin' on the bay
I want to be cruisin' like Nemo

No money but I wanna go far away
I don't have money but I wanna relax
No money but I wanna eat Jiro Ono's sushi
. . .
Woo there's no tomorrow
There's already a mortgage on my future
Woo spending my money even more
Friends, wussup
Do you want some?

— **BTS, "Go Go"**[128]

This song is a social commentary on the emptiness of the word *YOLO*, but at the same time, it also refers to how people "run" from reality and what truly matters. One fan interpretation pointed out the close connection between the word *dollar* in the song, and the Korean word 달려 (*dallyeo*), which means "run." The similar-sounding words point to the tendency of people to escape from harsh situations in life by mindlessly spending, or as one line says, "squandering fun." It's a lighthearted song that makes a strong point and asks listeners to take a hard look at themselves: "Leave me be, even if I overspend . . . Even if I break apart my savings tomorrow, like a crazy guy. For today, just go instead of worrying."

According to RM, the song tells the sad truth "about how our young generation are living their lives with low expectations and standards so people are upset with reality. We wanted to say something about it and emphasize to the world that it's not their choice, but [the] brutal reality that forces people to live and spend as if there's no future."

He continues, "In Korea, YOLO has become a big key word for young people because we don't have money and it's really hard to get a chance to earn a lot of money. That's the biggest luxury for Korea's young people: collecting accessories, cosmetics, that's what they think is a luxury. It's YOLO because it's like, 'I'm gonna buy all this! I'm gonna buy all this food and I'm going to eat it! I'm going to do it!' I think it's sad because it's all we can. 'Go Go' is just saying, 'Okay, just do it, we won't regret it. Just spend several bucks on the machine and eat the food!'"[129]

"SPRING DAY"

I miss you
When I say that
I miss you more
Even though I'm looking at your photo
I still miss you
Time is so cruel
I hate how things go between us
Now seeing each other for once is
So hard between us
It's all winter here

Even in August, it's all winter here
Time is gone by mind
Like a snowpiercer, I was left alone
I wanna hold your hand
And go to the other side of the earth
Wanna put an end this winter
How much do I have to long for you like
   snow piles up on the ground
Until the spring days come?
                    — BTS, "Spring Day"[130]

As Jungkook stands in a desolate theme park, one noticeable detail peeks from behind: yellow ribbons tied on the rails of an old, decrepit carousel. Every South Korean recognizes the yellow ribbon as a symbol of great significance, as it symbolizes the Sewol incident, a ferry disaster in 2014 that killed almost 300 passengers, the majority of them young students. The sinking of the ferry— which carried Danwon High School students on their way to a field trip on Jeju Island— shocked the whole nation to the core, with bereaved loved ones crying for justice and rallying against the government's indifference and glacial response. *The New York Times* reported that an association of student victims' families issued a statement on then-president Park Geun-hye's government regulatory failures, with some relatives accusing her of blocking an independent investigation into the causes of sinking and unsuccessful rescue efforts.[131] Reports said that the tragedy could've been prevented if safety measures were applied beforehand and if orderly evacuation and rescue were conducted.

What made the incident even more heartbreaking were the harrowing videos and text messages sent by the dead or missing victims before they disappeared into the sea. These were the only clues left from the youth that will never see the promise of their future. The tragedy is still clouded with mystery today.

"Mom, I might not be able to tell you in person. I love you," a text message read sent by a student to her mother before the ship capsized. A victim's father told news reporters, "Time has stopped. When I see students wearing school uniforms, I feel like my child will come back home and say, 'Dad, I'm home.'"

Years later, the little yellow ribbons still hang on keychains, cell phone accessories, and shop windows all over Korea, with sticker versions placed on cars, notebooks, and other items, reminding people to never forget that tragic day.

Although RM was quoted that their music video for "Spring Day" is open for interpretation, many viewers believe that it is one of the most heartfelt tributes to the disaster. In a press conference, the group was asked about the popularity of the video, with fans from across the world offering interpretations and explanations that connect it to the incident. "I'm careful to talk about the Sewol Ferry tragedy but as a citizen of the country, I do believe we should feel responsible. We thought we could send our condolences if we could," RM said, also mentioning a donation BTS made "to help the Sewol Ferry tragedy projects, psychology consultations for the victim families, etc."[132]

Some of the clues in the video were too coincidental to be considered just mere beautiful imagery. One of the crucial scenes was of member Jin, who was shown in a laundry room, with his image tilted as the water turned revealing him to be on the other side of the glass window of the washing machine. Perhaps this scene represents the grim image of the victims' bodies as they washed away under the sea.

Many fans explained that the recurring image of the clothes also represented the victims, and these were shown in one scene where pieces of clothing were floating in the water—and another when the BTS members were sitting on a huge mountain of clothes.

"Those abandoned suitcases and clothes represent all the students who went on their field trip with their belongings, and never came back," a YouTube account with the username "bulletproof vibes" wrote in a video explainer.[133]

Another important scene that could relate the whole video to the tragedy is when Jimin was holding a pair of sneakers while standing by the seashore. At the end of the video, the sneakers were shown hung and dangling on a branch of a tree. In some cultures, shoe flinging symbolizes bullying, a rite of passage, the end of a school year, or commemoration of the dead. In Korea, the families of the victims were left with only missing pairs of shoes or personal belongings of their dearly departed. A photo published by the AFP showed a shoe left at Jindo harbor by relatives of a victim and on the side of its soles is a message written: "My dear, your friend bought you a beautiful pair of shoes; your mum, sister and brother are all waiting for you."[134]

There were many other allusions in the video, but the last piece that completed the bigger picture was the fact that the tragedy happened in the spring, as the song title connotes. At the end of the video, cherry blossom petals that float in the air while the members walk toward the vast, empty fields symbolized the ephemerality of life. "Until this cold winter ends, and the Spring comes again. And until the flowers bloom again. Please stay there a little longer." The ending of the song gives hope that after misery, love, warmth, and happiness will come. "No darkness, no season, is forever."

"EPILOGUE: YOUNG FOREVER"

The curtain falls and I'm out of breath
I get mixed feelings as I breathe out
Did I make any mistakes today
How did the audience seem
I'm happy with who I've become
That I can make someone scream with joy

Still excited from the performance
I stand on the empty stage while holding onto
   an aftertaste that will not linger for long
While standing on this empty stage,
   I become afraid of this unpleasant
   emptiness
Within my suffocating feelings
On top of my life's line
Without a reason, I forcibly act that I am fine
This isn't the first time, I better get used to it
I try to hide it, but I can't
When the heat of the show cools down
I leave the empty seats behind

Trying to comfort myself
I tell myself the world can't be perfect
I start to let myself go
The thundering applause, I can't own it forever
I tell myself, so shameless
Raise your voice higher
Even if the attention isn't forever, I'll keep
   singing
As today's me, I want eternity
Forever, I want to be young
               — BTS, "EPILOGUE: YOUNG
                        FOREVER"[135]

While most of BTS's songs are drawn from vicarious experiences, literature, films, and current societal issues, the members of the band often find themselves opening up about their thoughts on fame and their struggle to come to peace with it. That is the core message of the song "Epilogue: Forever," where the lines vividly create a picture of the stage post-performance, long after the cheers have died down and the last fan has walked out of the venue. It goes on to describe the feeling of emptiness and the mixed feelings of joy about making other people happy, while on the inside, sadness grows as the moment of glory was only temporary.

This resonates with Suga the most, as he had written several songs about grappling with the pressures of achieving his dreams: "Anxiety and loneliness seem to be with me for life. I put a lot of meaning on how I would work it out, but it seems like I have to study it for my entire life. Emotions are so different in every situation and every moment, so I think to agonize every moment is what life is. By the lyrics, I wanted to tell people 'I am anxious, so are you, so let's find the way and study the way together.'"[136]

He says he still has a long way to go, but by opening himself and expressing his worries creatively, he was able to find acceptance and some calm from the fast-paced celebrity life that he now lives. "Now I don't feel like I'm running for a specific dream, but these days I started to think that values and happiness as a person are important."

RM also shared the same thoughts as Suga, referring to his anxiety as a "shadow that grows into the night."

In the video, the members were shown separated and trapped inside a maze. No matter how much they run, they couldn't find the way out. This seems to imply the constant worries that run inside their heads; the more they try to escape it, the more they end up back to where they came from. As they go through the maze alone, all their fears and feelings of loneliness come to haunt them.

The pitfalls of fame and its inevitable psychological toll on its seekers is a story that has been told by many young artists like BTS. But in Korea, this is still considered taboo, and the group has sought ways to change this by being honest about their feelings. In an interview, Jimin expressed that he once "felt lonely realizing that there is no one to understand me when a hard time comes."[137]

The other message of the song is their journey to adulthood, and even though they have to face bigger responsibilities, they want to look back and cherish their beautiful memories of youth.

The endings of most, if not all, of their videos are hopeful. Changing the dark gray tones to warm hues that come with the sunset, the last scenes of "Young Forever" offer reconciliation and tranquility as an alternative to the tumult inside their heads. They run free from the maze and find each other. As RM said, the members, his friends, and family become his "resting place" that helps him "shorten the distance between me and the world."

For BTS, to be "young forever" meant staying grounded and finding joy in simple things. To keep running fearlessly toward a dream, just like a child.

"BLOOD, SWEAT, AND TEARS"

My blood, sweat, and tears
My last dance too
Take it all away

My blood, sweat, and tears
My cold breath too
Take it all away
My blood, sweat, and tears
— BTS, "Blood, Sweat, and Tears"[138]

IN HIS SEARCH FOR THE MEANING OF BEING, French philosopher Gabriel Marcel wrote, "to truly confront mystery, one must open themselves up to the avenues designed for this purpose—religion, art, and metaphysics."

BTS's video for "Blood, Sweat, and Tears" took their audiences into an odyssey of the mystery of the self, with a sophisticated, highly stylized, and complicated music video that is riddled with artistic imagery where they chartered into the religious, mythological, and philosophical territories. They peel the layers of human experience with every little detail: from the metaphors of good and evil, Renaissance paintings in the background, the inscription on the walls, iconography, statues, and Biblical references, down to the roles that each of the members play.

The whole plot of the video was inspired by the book, *Demian: The Story of Emil Sinclair's Youth*, written by Hermann Hesse. It tells the story of a young boy as he is caught in between two worlds: reality and illusion, heaven and hell. This was brought to life in the video, with symbolism sewn into the scenes. One member bites into an apple, another one struggles to break free while blindfolded, all of the members gather on a table, portraying "The Last Supper" by Leonardo da Vinci, and so much more. The most significant element in the video is black angel wings on V's back and on a statue, which both refer to a character in the book and the title of their fourth studio album, *Wings*.

The video touches upon the reflection on the mystery of being, and the desire for transcendence, meaning, coherence, and truth. One must watch it in order to see these nuances and understand that there is more to the aesthetically pleasing aspect of the costumes, choreography, and psychedelic graphics. RM narrates during a moving scene in the video: "He too was a tempter; he, too, was a link to the second, the evil world with which I no longer wanted to have anything to do."

It alludes to the inner battle of a free-spirited youth coming to terms with the loss of innocence and falling into sin and temptation. It's a revolt against the illusions of happiness, love, and peace—and in order to understand these values, one must undergo despair, darkness, and downfall. All of these, while leading to self-destruction, are necessary for the awakening and realization of the self, as is the central message of *Demian*, which was influenced by existential philosophers Friedrich Nietzsche and Carl Jung.

Fans have dissected the video and discussed its many possible meanings in online forums, with one fan commenting that a university course on BTS could be a fun addition to education. Observers also noted that BTS ignited among fans a whole new interest in literature, particularly the books featured in their concepts.

"I enjoyed reading *Demian* when I was young. It was cool and difficult, but I went to read it again after knowing the concept of the *Wings* album. It's a coming-of-age novel and we tried our best to portray it," RM, who co-wrote the titular song with Suga and J-Hope, said in an interview about the album.

"ANSWER: LOVE MYSELF," "21ST CENTURY GIRL," AND "CYPHER PT. 4"

"I STARTED DEALING WITH ANXIETY AND PANIC disorder but their music has helped me get through them and honestly they're the reason I am who I am today. I am much more smiley than I used to be," one fan said during an interview with BBC outside BTS's concert venue in London's O2 Arena in 2018. Another fan shared how she learned to embrace her flaws, idiosyncrasies, and self-doubt after listening to BTS's album, *Love Yourself: Answer*, aptly titled as though it was offering advice to anyone who needs it.

Loving myself might be harder
Than loving someone else
Let's admit it
The standards I made are more strict for
    myself
The thick tree rings in your life
It's part of you, it's you
Now let's forgive ourselves
Our lives are long, trust yourself when in a
    maze
When winter passes, spring always comes
. . .
The me of yesterday, the me of today, the
    me of tomorrow
(I'm learning how to love myself)
With no exceptions, it's all me
. . .
Yes, I have that beauty
Knowing that is going
On the path to loving myself

It's what I need the most
I'm walking for myself
It's an action needed for me
My attitude towards myself
That's the happiness I need for me
    — BTS, "Answer: Love Yourself"[139]

Throughout their career, BTS has always tried to make everything positive, or at least help fans see the brighter side of an otherwise bleak situation. They look at what's happening around them and offer a dual course of perspectives: hopeful but not idealistic, aggressive but not violent, realistic but not cynical. Whether it's political, personal, or an intellectual discourse, the underlying meanings in their songs may seem daunting at first, but in the grand scheme of things, BTS has but one resounding message—love yourself.

Their song "21st Century Girl" has become an anthem for empowering women, with BTS singing, "Whatever other people say, whatever this world tells you . . . Tell them that you're strong, tell them you're enough. You're the best to me just the way you are."

Perhaps this is the greatest contribution of their music: to become an inner voice of encouragement, pride, and self-acceptance for anyone who's willing to listen. As the repeating rap lines in "Cypher Pt. 4" goes: "I love I love I love myself, I know I know I know myself."

The simple yet weighty verses encapsulate the heart, phases, and culmination of their *Love Yourself* series albums: to acknowledge one's weaknesses, faults, and mistakes in the past, to forgive, to let go, and, finally, love oneself. As in "Answer's" poignant line, "Me, who used to be sad, me, who used to be hurt, it'll make me more beautiful."

The series—which comprised of *Love Yourself: Her*, *Love Yourself: Wonder*, *Love Yourself: Tear*, and finally, *Love Yourself: Answer*—presents the proverbial way of storytelling. They are made up of an introduction, a twist, and conclusion, all completed with the necessary chapters telling the narrative of falling in love, loss or separation, and learning lessons along the way. Their songs convey the catharsis of this life process, and in the end, only when one has been emptied of insecurities, heartbreak, and anger, can they fully love the self and the other.

In July 2019, BTS released the LOVE MYSELF Global Campaign video, which shows young victims of violence who found comfort and courage by listening to BTS's music. It is part of the band's advocacy to help the youth to heal and inspire them to find the light within themselves.

CHAPTER 10

THE PROBLEMATIC MEDIA PORTRAYAL AND PERCEPTION OF BTS

BTS at the American Music Awards.

"ASIAN ONE DIRECTION." "THE KOREAN Beatles."[140] "Asians with bowl cuts." These are only a few examples of the name-calling and negative remarks BTS were met with on Twitter when they were promoting in the US and in other non-Asian countries. It was almost the same treatment given to the many Korean artists who preceded them. Korean singer Rain, who toured in the US in 2006 was called "the Asian Justin Timberlake," while BoA was dubbed as the "Korean Britney Spears" when she debuted with her self-titled English album in the US in 2008. And it doesn't apply only to Korean

acts. Terms like "American crossover" or "Western takeover" are often used to depict certain artists' promotional activities. They are sometimes introduced as "foreign exports."

"There's an underlying assumption that it's only natural for English-speaking artists to go global, perform on world tours, and top charts in dozens of countries," Aamina Khan writes for *Teen Vogue*. "No one would ever question why singers like Shawn Mendes and Justin Bieber, both Canadian, receive such overwhelming success in non-English-speaking countries and are taken seriously as artists by the media and the general public."[141]

Much has been said about the proclivity of the West to contain or at least give meaning to something new by associating it with something similar. In order to understand an individual or a group—that is from another country, speaks a different language, looks a certain way, or deviates from long-established Western standards—they are often connected to people or concepts that are more familiar. This happens even when they are total opposites or have just a few similarities with the object of comparison. But this tendency goes beyond preferences and certainly reveals more than just a simple way of trying to process new information. Restricting artists within the confines of labels often limits the public perception of what that artist can offer. It opens up the possibility of treating the subject with stereotypes, or worse, promoting racism and xenophobia under the guise of satire and wit. One expert regarded it as a way to understand the unfamiliar, while many observers note that it all comes down to prejudice and mere disregard for different cultures, beliefs, and opinions.

South Korean music critic and author of *BTS: The Review; A Comprehensive Look at the Music of BTS*, Kim Youngdae told *The Atlantic*, "The American mainstream music industry is really hesitant to call Asian artists 'pop stars.' They're okay with characterizing them as a subculture, or as an Asian American movement. But the entertainment industry always has to acknowledge the hottest or biggest thing, whether they like it or not."

Several fans often notice when coverage or interviews about BTS seem problematic. For instance, a profile feature about BTS on *The Hollywood Reporter* angered fans for calling BTS a "virtual mystery"[142] when "BTS has been covered by almost every major media outlet, and they are arguably the most popular band in the world right now,"[143] as author Frederick Joseph tweeted in response to the writer's defense online. Fans also criticized the unpreparedness of the writer who confessed at the beginning of his article, "I admit to being a little fuzzy on some of the finer points of BTS history, like where they came from, why they are so appealing to so many millions or even what BTS stands for."[144]

BTS also fit the stereotype of boy bands, which is perhaps why they tend to become the subject of jokes and insensitive comments online. They have good-looking members, synchronized choreography, well-coordinated costumes, and have legions of young female fans.

"When Americans see the handsome boys dancing together, for them that's obviously the format of the boy band. But for Korean people and for fans, they're more like a hip-hop group with vocal abilities who can also dance supremely well . . . For a lot of people, 'boy band' would automatically discount their musical ability and authenticity," Kim explained.[145]

This brings us to another big problem: how many people from the West react when they see BTS, a boy band by technical standards, at prestigious award shows where other

"Today we are making history," RM once told the members before going on stage.

world-renowned artists gather. Whether as special guests, presenters, or recipients of an award, BTS being invited to big events such as the Billboard Music Awards, the Grammys, and the American Music Awards indicates a huge boon to their career. But not everybody thinks so. These responses have since been deleted on Twitter, but not before fans were able to take screen shots and call them out. *The Huffington Post* compiled some of these tweets, in an article titled "Billboard Music Awards 2017: Backlash over BTS win proves how racist people can be."[146]

- "[I don't even know] who those Asians were. I don't wanna know. I'm baffled. I didn't understand what they said. Award shows are so trash now."
- "Not trying to be racist, but you don't see any American singer or band participating in a Korean award show so, like, BTS please just go back to Korea."
- "K-Pop is still irrelevant, nobody in the States is gonna listen to a Korean song just because BTS won an award."[147]

One of the most talked about shows that received a mountain of backlash after portraying BTS in a negative slant is a countdown segment about "Greatest Global Crazes" on Channel 9, one of Australia's major TV networks. The hosts and celebrity

At the 61st Annual Grammy Awards, RM addressed the crowd alongside BTS: "Growing up in South Korea, we always dreamed of being on the Grammys stage." "Thank you all our fans for making this dream come true and we'll be back."

guests each took turns reviewing BTS, which was first introduced as "the biggest band you've never heard of."

Comedian from the UK Jimmy Carr referenced North Korea and its controversial leader, saying, "Kim Jong Un is well into boy bands. When I first heard something Korean had exploded in America, I got worried, so I guess it could have been worse. But not much worse."[148]

One personality in the show made fun of their "gangster names," while another made a snide comment, saying, "There's seven of them, that is too high cast, surely you could fire four of them, then you can hire a sedan and have nice leg room." The show even went on to ridicule a monumental moment for BTS when RM delivered a speech in the UN, pertaining to it instead as a "talk about hair products."

In the American entertainment program *E! News*, the host and two news correspondents discussed the backlash received by the MTV Video Music Awards (VMAs) for creating a separate K-pop category. The issue is that a separate category disregards the achievements of BTS, who have record album sales and critical acclaim, which should make them equals to other Western artists. It is also a question of credibility in the qualifying standards for the categories set by the show's organizing executives. For instance, K-pop group Monsta X was also nominated in the K-pop category, but their song "Who Do You Love" featuring French Montana

was entirely in English. This created another problematic issue that was also experienced by the artists nominated for the Latin category: Were Korean artists put in one category simply because they are Koreans?

But one correspondent vehemently argued in favor of the separate category, explaining, "We in America didn't name K-pop, 'K-pop.' It's a specific genre of music. In order to be a K-pop artist, you gotta go to a K-pop college and that's a real thing. There's a certain fanatic to it, dance style . . ." He also claimed that there are certain interest groups that lobby for K-pop artists to be included in award shows, while the main host said that it was made to "satisfy BTS fans because they're loud and proud."

Only one correspondent spoke on the side of ARMYs: "I think they've really missed the mark with BTS by putting them in a separate category. It's not necessarily racist to have their own category but it's a way to avoid having them in the main categories. I don't know why they didn't acknowledge their achievements."

E! News has since removed the video online, but some internet users were able to keep a copy of the clip.

The hashtags #VMAsRacist and #VMAsAreOverParty trended on Twitter after the MTV VMA's announcement of the new category, Best of K-Pop. BTS fans pointed out that the band is not up for major categories such as Video of the Year, Artist of the Year, and Best New Artist. Fans called out VMAs online for using a photo centered on Halsey's face to represent the "Boy With Luv" collaboration rather than a photo that features BTS.[149]

In the end, BTS did win the controversial VMA for Best K-pop group for their song "Boy With Luv," though a report in *Variety* notes, "It's not hard to see why the move generated controversy. After all, BTS' accomplishments have matched or outpaced many American, Canadian and Australian nominees, who weren't exiled to a nationality-based category."[150]

On their end, BTS and their agency remained silent on most, if not all, of the instances involving controversy, but a few of the members have indirectly mentioned them. RM shared about their experience at the American Music Awards, saying, "The AMAs didn't treat us as a curious novelty from Asia, but showed us respect and treated us as an important part of the show."[151] When industry observers compared the achievements and fan pandemonium sparked by BTS with "Beatlemania" in the 1960s, Suga addressed this, saying, "Although it's an honor to be named the 21st century Beatles, we want to be the 21st century BTS."

David Tizzard from the *Korea Times* offered another perspective when he wrote an opinion piece titled "Korea, Racism, and BTS,"[152] justifying that the jokes calling attention to the band are another form of exposure and that it is actually advantageous to them. He started off by recognizing the band's commercial clout, but that "with such success comes the inevitable satire and parodies. Of course, comedians and entertainers generally use the most popular and well-known of cultural references for their jokes . . . because otherwise no-one would get them."

He wrote further, "So, the fact that BTS are now the subject of light-hearted observations on Australian TV is, if anything, testament to their growing popularity and global achievements."

With regard to the ARMYs' reaction, he claimed, "They were just upset that something they love, and perhaps see as an extension of the country itself, could be treated so flippantly by people abroad. But the calling of the jokes 'racist' and 'xenophobic' is the problem. And it's a problem because it then clouds the water as to when something is actually racist or xenophobic."

The gist of his rhetoric was summed up in one of the lines in his article, "The comedy was not designed to separate, segregate, or demean. Conversely, it was demonstrating that South Korean pop culture is now worthy of being joked about at the international level."

Consistent with his stance on his previous article, he wrote another one titled "BTS vs Dave," in which he wrote, "Despite the cries of racism and xenophobia rising up from the internet about this nascent K-pop category—I personally think it's something of which South Korea as a country should be very proud."[153]

Unlike Tizzard's piece, which focused on the Western media's facetious and often not-so serious response to BTS, writer Erica

Russel highlighted the opposite. In her article for mtv.com, titled, "Why do critics love Bong Joon Ho and dismiss BTS?" she called out critics for taking the *Parasite* director seriously and not the group, even when "the Korean virtuosos both make vital, thought-provoking art."[154]

Directed by Bong Joon Ho, the Korean-language film *Parasite* won four Academy Awards at the 2020 Oscars, becoming the first non-English language film in Oscar history to win the award for Best Picture.[155]

While BTS and Bong Joon Ho have different types of artistry, they share similarities aside from being Koreans. The group and the director share a common thread, particularly their predilection for exploring dark, socio-political themes. The director has been making provocative films for more than two decades, with his most recent creation *Parasite* capturing international acclaim for its humorous, gruesome, and bizarre depiction of the divide between the rich and the poor. Its universal message was deemed by audiences as relevant not only to South Korea but also the whole world, which made the film a box office success locally and internationally. BTS, on the other hand, has been writing and singing songs about capitalism, youth activism, and other societal issues, as discussed in Chapter 9 of this book. How the Western media views BTS and the *Parasite* creator, however, is an entirely different story, with many critics tending to favor the latter rather than the former. Russell wrote, "attempting to ignore either's impact on pop culture would prove an absurd exercise in either delusion, if not willful exclusion."

BTS and Bong Joon Ho's works open important conversations through music and film, both in their messages and imagery. Their works seem to speak to many different audiences because they're often inspired by reality. "In doing so, both are disrupting entertainment media on a global scale. Whether intentionally or subsequently, BTS and Bong are challenging the outdated, largely white perceptions of Asian media in the West. They're also normalizing Asian representation, period," Russell stressed.

It is only now that the world is taking notice of them, but unfortunately, "Many U.S. critics have labeled Bong's film as a masterpiece. But BTS's music—even the group's most well-received, expertly crafted albums—remains unfairly relegated to pop culture fluff by many seasoned critics."

Interviewed in the same article, journalist Kim Jae Ha also noted that, "Given that he's a middle-aged man [Bong Joon Ho] who looks more like an average Korean man than a celebrity, no one is going to accuse him of being famous simply because of his looks. With BTS, many people assume they're an overnight sensation. The average person doesn't realize they've been a group for the past seven years and worked diligently on their artistry before they ever became famous."

"Boy bands aren't respected in general and that's because they're viewed as teenybopper bands that only little girls like," Kim continued, "It's such a sexist and outdated viewpoint . . . Mainstream Western audience has never been kind to most boy bands, so I'm not surprised that they're dismissive of BTS." Aside from the already skewed perception of boy bands, racism also plays a detrimental role when it comes to the portrayal of BTS. "The fact that they're Korean just adds fuel to the fire for racists who view Asian men as inferior."

The stereotype that BTS fans are all composed of naive and young "teenyboppers" can be proven inaccurate once statistics and data are considered. According to ticketing marketplace Vivid Seat, fans who bought concert tickets for "Love Yourself: Speak Yourself" have shown both growth in demand and diversity in terms of age.[156] ARMYs are made up of people from different backgrounds, race, professions, ages, genders, and the like.

A fan posted in an AllKpop forum about how she feels when ARMYs are described as superficial fans: "A large group of us have some substance, thank you very much, and are decently intelligent. I think,

if anything, being a BTS fan can often be a good indicator of one's intelligence due to the creativity, depth, and sharpness of the insights reflected in their work about life. That is completely overlooking BTS' ability to produce penetrating and thoughtful work that resonates to a more matured, well-educated fan base."[157]

Even the *Parasite* director acknowledged BTS's huge impact. During a red carpet interview at the Golden Globes 2020, Bong Joon Ho praised the group, saying, "Although I'm here at the Golden Globes, BTS has three thousand times the amount of power and influence [than] I have. I think Korea produces a lot of great artists 'cause we're very emotionally dynamic people."[158]

It would be ideal if one of the lines of his acceptance speech for winning the Golden Globe award for Best Foreign Language Film was also applied to music: "Once you overcome the one-inch-tall barrier of subtitles, you will be introduced to so many more amazing films."

In the same way, Suga told American teen magazine *J-14*, "You will like BTS music if you listen to it without prejudice."

BTS

CHAPTER 11

THE REAL AND PERSONAL STORY OF ARMYS

The author of this book interviewed BTS fans from different parts of the world via email and asked two questions: How did they discover BTS? What songs changed their lives? The following is a compilation of stories written by the fans themselves, explaining their journey of how they have come to know and love BTS.

BTS IS A GOOD ROLE MODEL FOR MY CHILDREN

SHELLIE HANSEN, 46, DENMARK

I became ARMY by accident!

My daughter was twelve at the time (early 2018) and had become close to our babysitter, who was fifteen, and very much into BTS and K-pop. She was often at our house and would talk our ears off about BTS, who they were, and what they stood for, but she had also talked about other Korean artists, as well as others such as Ariana Grande, who I've never gotten into so I'm not sure when or how it all occurred. At some point, BTS became the group we heard about most, and as they started to watch more music videos at home while we were all together, I began to see and hear them. I am naturally interested in what my children and their friends do and like, so I watched and listened. I thought some of the songs were "fun" and videos quite different, colorful, artistic and dramatic, but simply thought, "Okay, so this is my daughter's thing. Cool, I get it, but it's not my music." Then they started putting the subtitles on and I saw what they were singing about and became intrigued. I started listening more closely to what the girls were talking about. I even watched a couple of "reality" videos on YouTube, clips of them doing silly things, and a V-Live.

After a few months, I said something about V, and maybe one of the others, and my daughter turned to me and said, "Mum, you're ARMY now!" It's bonding us at an important time in her life as she's becoming a teenager.

From there, I somehow managed to learn all their names and started to enjoy their message and songs quite a bit. I studied psychology and philosophy at university, which played a part in my interest. I'd decided after seeing them in Run, V-Live,

©Shellie Hansen

and interviews that they were the type of role models I'd like for my children. My son, who is three years younger than his sister, had in the meantime also started listening to K-pop and was singing in Korean to himself. Around the same time, we started watching a lot of Asian dramas at home.

I saw finally that these "idols" were the type I hadn't known existed. BTS on the other hand seemed genuine, down to earth, humble, honest. I could appreciate and enjoy that my children were into these types of people and singers. It was no longer just about the music.

I have to backtrack to say that my children are half-Filipino (racially) and half-Danish. Due to my upbringing (long story), I've never felt "sufficiently" Asian, never truly been proud to be Asian, I'm ashamed to say. All of a sudden, I could see my children seeing Asian men/boys that they thought were cool, attractive, beautiful, what have you—and it became even more important. They cheered every success; my daughter now feels pride and gets excited whenever we see Asian people. (We live in a very monocultural country). She now goes to Korean and Mandarin classes, and our future travel plans and goals have changed significantly. BTS also introduced us to other Korean and Eastern artists.

I tried to get concert tickets for Europe in October 2018. Even though I tried for London, Paris, Amsterdam, and Berlin, it didn't work out as I wasn't prepared to pay over a certain amount "just" for concert

tickets. That attitude changed by 2019.

2019 has seen the three of us with every BTS and BT21 related app, with me rejoining Twitter, first to follow for my daughter, and now for myself. I'm part of a BTS ARMY mothers group on Facebook, and have connected with ARMY of all ages near and far, mostly on social media but also in real life. It makes me slightly emotional to write about it. ARMY is about and for the seven boys and their music, but it is also a community, which is for the most part a respectful, varied, intelligent, and comforting "family" to be a part of.

After a very stressful experience, we managed to get tickets for Wembley Day One. We've been to London many times as a family and I've lived there previously, but those few days were a BTS world, going to different events, buying merchandise, meeting up with ARMY we'd mostly only known online and of course, the concert. We went three hours early, as did others. I can't describe the feeling of excitement and camaraderie in being at a concert without the "band" there and everyone already singing along, dancing and having fun.

I listen to BTS every day and have for at least the last six months. There's not a song I don't like although there are songs for different moods. My favorite ones are "Singularity," "Stigma," "Begin," and "Pied Piper," so there seems to be a type of sound there. I love all the rap mixtapes too. I really hesitate to say I have a favorite as I don't know if I do.

I think of these boys as my family, extra

sons or nephews or something. I feel a closeness and love for them that I've never had for any artist or actor, no matter how much I liked their work. They let us in and give to us in a completely different way, in a dialogue.

Needless to say, I'm ARMY for life, and I believe my children will be too, but that remains to be seen. And with being ARMY, that brings it with a continued interest in Korea and its culture and people—continuing Korean classes for us, films, drama, cultural events, literature, food, beauty products, and travel.

©Shellie Hansen

BTS: A GENDER TRANSITION OST

AIDEN HOBBS, 40, USA

©SAiden Hobbs

My journey to becoming a BTS fan and proud ARMY has its own plot twist. I moved to Korea in 2009 and embraced K-pop almost immediately like many other expats. The first groups I listened to were typical and included 2NE1, 4Minute, TVXQ, Super Junior, BIG BANG, and f(x) among many others. While each of these groups were uniquely fantastic, YouTube brought BTS to me and the first song I remember hearing from them was "Born Singer," a cover track of "Born Sinner" by J. Cole. This song was so honest and raw even though it was by a K-pop group and a rewritten cover of a rap/R&B song that speaks to the struggle of a black man who strives to rise above his transgressions. It was a surprise to me to find BTS to be so genuinely talented and sincerely self-expressive.

Learning about the members and their stories resonated with me more than other groups because the young men of BTS reflected my perceptions of balanced masculinity and the essence of brotherhood. I wanted to explore my gender identity to embody a more masculine representation. In them, I could see some of the puzzle pieces of my buried persona. I wanted to be true to myself, even if it scared me and I wasn't sure if people were going to understand or accept me. In 2014, I started seeking counseling to better address this turmoil that

had blindsighted (sic) me. I was a 35-year-old, self-identified boyish lesbian, and a person of color expat who was teaching at a countryside university. What was going to happen if I stood up for my right to evolve into a more authentic representation of myself? Do I erase all that I was or find a way to merge my past with who I wanted to be? I took each step slowly and clung to the messages of BTS as my anchor while embracing new dimensions of masculine and feminine energy that lay dormant within for far too long.

To me, they are the friends that I didn't have in real life because we can't turn back the hands of time to reset our gendered social experiences. I couldn't undo my female-bodied experiences nor was learning to live as a male-bodied person going to be easy. I could, however, start where I was and continue forward towards self-love, acceptance, and living out loud. BTS taught me to value the journey no matter where it starts or what may lie ahead. They showed me that masculinity is not limited to Western standards and that being quirky, compassionate, creative, sensitive, emotional, or effeminate are all valid human qualities to embody no matter your gender or gender expression. My duality is my strength and I have to love myself for the journey my body, mind, and spirit have been on. Although, all of the members show incredible tenacity, passion, and wisdom beyond their years, Park Jimin will forever be my bias and mentor in being strong, vulnerable, self-critical, and driven to push through personal challenges. His dancing ability constantly unnerves and provokes my artistic sensibilities.

My favorite song is nearly impossible to choose but I will say that "Not Today," "4 O'Clock," "Do You," and "Magic Shop" are among my top favorites. I think "Not Today" and "Do You" help me when I need to feel strong and lift myself out of periodic states of depression and anxiety. They remind me of just how much I have already overcome in life and that going backwards is not an option. "4 O'Clock" and "Magic Shop" reassure me that everyone can feel lonely and unloved but we are never really alone nor are we unlovable. ARMY is increasingly diverse and encourages people to speak up

©SAiden Hobbs

©SAiden Hobbs

©SAiden Hobbs

I am not a young ARMY member but I am proud to be one. I am not heteronormative in my gender expression or sexuality but I stand strong in my trans experience. The mutual respect that BTS and ARMY have for each other continues to ignite hope and compassion worldwide. While I have not been able to show my appreciation to them directly via fansigns or other events, I am always trying to support them in other ways. If they ever see this, I want to say this: "Thank you for always holding true to your values under great pressure, expectations, and scrutiny. You brought light into a very dark place in my life and for that I commend you. No matter where the journey takes each of you as life unfolds in different directions, stay grounded in who you are as men of talent and honor. As an international ARMY, I am never going to stop fighting for the power to speak for myself and others like me who can't take off their masks to allow for others to see their light."

and connect with others. Sharing joy with a global community feels like you have a chosen family that unites in perseverance, understanding, and supersedes cultural boundaries.

A PROUD ARMY FOR LIFE

MARIAH HARPER, 28, USA

I first got into BTS when I was working in China as a teacher in February 2018. My friend and coworker asked if I was into K-pop and I told her I never listened to it before. She recommended I listen to BTS and I instantly fell in love. I first got hooked on their choreography as I used to be a dancer. I loved watching their dance practices!

I binge-watched all their music videos and *Run BTS* episodes as well as any variety shows they were on or interviews.

I loved their message as I got into them during their *Love Yourself* series but I loved listening to all of their old songs too. I listened to all their songs while reading the English translations. My favorite song is "Spring Day."

It has such a melancholic feel to it and I cry almost every time I listen to it. When RM dropped his solo album *Mono*, I really felt connected to his song "Seoul." It made me miss my hometown, but also made me feel free and glad to have moved.

While living in China I was able to get tickets to their *Love Yourself* tour in Canada. I was so excited to finally see them live! I met up with some friends I only talked to on the internet and we had the best time ever!

BTS has changed my life because I have a strong feeling of wanting to make them proud. Even though I know I'll probably never meet them, I want to live a good, full life and always love myself. Being their fan I want to live a life that they would be proud of: by always following my heart and my dreams.

I've also met some amazing lifetime

©Mariah Harper

©Mariah Harper

©Mariah Harper

©Mariah Harper

©Mariah Harper

friends through BTS. They feel like my real-life friends. I can see a little part of myself in all of them. I truly think they are the funniest people ever. Whenever I'm feeling stressed or down I'll watch my favorite *Run* episodes to laugh 'til I cry. Or I'll learn a new dance from them. Or when I need a good cry I'll put on my Chill Bangtan playlist and just let it all out.

I'm so happy to have them in my life and I'm so thankful to my friend for introducing me. It makes me so emotional to think that I'm living in the same time as BTS. They are going to be written in history and I'm so excited to witness it! I'm in this for life!

©Mariah Harper

BTS UPLIFTED MY SPIRIT
MARIEL AGUINALDO, PHILIPPINES

I started listening to K-pop around ten years ago. It was very casual: I didn't get into the culture, didn't even search the meanings of the songs, just picked up songs here and there as long as I liked the sound.

When BTS's "Idol" came out, my brother asked me to listen to it. Truthfully, I wasn't very impressed, and I didn't even give the song another spin. But then he showed me BTS's performance of "Mic Drop Remix" on *Jimmy Kimmel*, and I absolutely loved it.

It was so elegant but also had the right touch of ruggedness. The choreography was amazing too, so powerful and confident. I remember being so impressed not only by their synchronicity but also their charm and stage presence, qualities that you can't just find in any act. This video was on loop for me for days on end; I could not get enough of their performance.

During my commute to work, I randomly decided to listen to their album, *Love Yourself: Answer*. The moment "Euphoria's" lilting notes hit my ears, I was taken aback. By the time I finished listening to the album, I was absolutely stunned. Every song was beautiful, every sound different, and most importantly, I felt the soul in them. You could almost touch the thoughtfulness in every note, the love and labor that went into their craft. From that moment on, I declared myself an ARMY.

There are so many reasons to like BTS,

©Mariel Aguinaldo

the main one being their music. These are the songs that resonated with me: "Seesaw," which comforted me during a crisis in a relationship; "Awake" that had me sobbing because of how it captured my being so entirely; *Mono*, which calms me the moment the city sounds of "Tokyo" begin playing. It's music that's meant to stir our depths and awaken us from our slumber.

I can talk about the boys' charming personalities, their absolute love for ARMY that makes them so open and comfortable with us. I can attribute it to their kind hearts, how they've risen against prejudice in so many ways: singing about oppression, learning from negative experiences, and inspiring generosity. Suga's words awakened me, "The bigger the dream, the better," and RM spoke to me with, "Eventually fools change the world." Their words sparked life back into my jaded self. They taught me to lift my head high and start dreaming again.

Somebody once said that you know you love someone when you can't pinpoint the exact reason why you do—and that's precisely how I feel about BTS. It's this very same love that I'll treasure deep in my heart, knowing that seven boys from South Korea gave me so much and only expect my sincere love in return.

BTS INSPIRED ME TO FOLLOW MY DREAM
CJ WIRTH, 30, USA

©CJ Wirth

I got to know BTS through a friend in November 2016 during the *Wings* era. I hadn't talked to her in a while and she suddenly contacted me because she wanted to "catch up" so I suggested we go out for lunch but she invited me to her house instead and she forced me to watch a bunch of BTS videos. I officially caved in on December 13, 2016 and I thought it would just be a passing phase, but two-and-a-half years later I'm still devoted to them. I love them so much because they stand out from not only other K-pop groups but also other artists in general. BTS has their own unique style and their lyrics have important meanings. They also realize that their fans come from different cultures, backgrounds, and convictions and they don't do anything or write anything that excludes a certain class of people. I also love them because they are talented, funny, hardworking, and completely devoted to their fans. They inspired me to follow my dreams. My dream since I was eighteen was to teach English in Asia and ten years later I finally got around to doing it, and now I'm teaching English in South Korea at a school that I love.

©CJ Wirth

©CJ Wirth

BTS TAUGHT ME ABOUT KOREA

SHRUTIKA SINHA, 24, INDIA

©Shrutika Sinha

I first got to know BTS in 2016 while I was watching some videos on YouTube. But I did not become an ARMY back then. I was just listening to their music and enjoyed it. But then at the end of 2017 when I got the news that I will be moving to South Korea to further my studies, I wanted to learn a little bit about Korean language and culture, and I thought, "What better way to learn it than music?"

I started paying attention to their lyrics more and my love for them grew, and now here I am loving BTS every single second of my life. I like them because of the music and the message they spread. They taught me how to find happiness in little things. They taught me that if I work hard I can achieve anything in life.

There are so many songs that moved me and I have cried and smiled because of them, which is why I can't decide which song touched me the most. So I will just say that BTS's songs have a relatable message that reaches out to everyone. They themselves are very relatable. They inspire me every day.

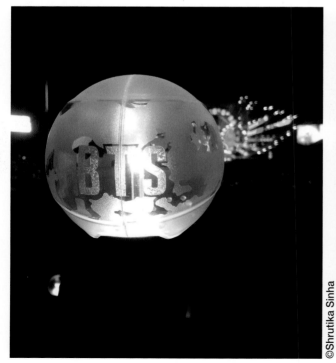

©Shrutika Sinha

©Shrutika Sinha

BTS IS A WHOLE FAMILY AFFAIR

JOSH AND CAIT MURISAN, 30 AND 29, USA

We are from the YouTube channel called Murisan Family Vlogs, where we post video reactions to BTS contents. We got into BTS from our six-year-old daughter Zoey. One day she was on her iPad and we heard BTS playing. We wanted to bond with her in a different way than our parents did with us and showed our interest in her passion and what she enjoys. Turns out she was playing *Roblox* and was in a BTS part of the game. That night we looked them up and there was a recent video of them on *SNL* performing so we reacted to it. It was amazing! The music moved me in ways even with the language barriers. ARMYs commented on more of our videos and welcomed us in the ARMY family. We haven't missed a day since then.

©Josh and Cait Murisan

Our love for them grew very quickly when we went to their concert at the Metlife Stadium in New Jersey on May 2019. We bought BT21 merchandise within moments. We were hooked. The music enabled us to open up and talk to people all around the world. My husband Josh loves "Euphoria" and he could relate the lyrics with our family. I love "Epiphany" by Jin because it moves my heart, but so does every song we hear. Our journey is amazing and we thank the ARMY for guiding the way and showing us all the sides of BTS. They came into our lives when we needed them the most. They not only filled us with happiness but also strengthened the bond between our family, and our family also grew when we met the ARMYs.

©Josh and Cait Murisan

NEVER TOO YOUNG OR OLD TO BE A BTS FAN

RAFRANZ DAVIS, 44, USA

I've always been active on Twitter because of my career but leading up to the AMA's in 2017, I started noticing the hashtags that referred to their performance. They trended every single day. After I finally saw them perform, I was hooked, and the rest is history.

I love the honesty in their lyrics and how they treat art as fearless as we should all see the world. If there was any significant change in my life, it would have to be that I no longer spend 95 percent of my time dedicated to work only. I now take the time to enjoy moments with my family, community, and doing things that I love outside of work. I travel for fun now which is new to me.

The song that has moved me most is "Tomorrow." I feel encouraged to keep dreaming and working for what I want, even at 44 years young. You're never too old to be a BTS fan and their music has encouraged me in ways that I could not have imagined possible.

©Rafranz Davis

On a more personal level, the love and support of BTS is something that has brought my entire family together. We gather to watch their live events as a family, attend their movies, and even travel to watch their concerts. This is a first for our family and we will love BTS forever for bringing us together in this way.

BTS'S MUSIC HEALS AND COMFORTS

ASHLEY CRUZ, 27, PHILIPPINES

Before BTS, I was uninterested with anything K-pop-related despite having friends and cousins who are into it. It's not something new to me but it's also not my cup of tea. I don't understand the lyrics and I honestly had a preconceived notion that they all sound the same.

©Ashley Cruz

I already had BTS under my radar because they're always trending but I never really checked them out. I remained unbothered and uninterested. Until the morning of October 2018, I woke up to a clip uploaded by *The Graham Norton Show*, which is one of my favorites. I watched the interview first, then their "Idol" live stage. I thought they were really good live so I went to YouTube and watched more videos, until I found myself watching every video that I found.

It wasn't their message that got me into them at first, but the way they put up a great show; their intense choreography, and stable voices. Then I made an effort to know more about them. As I went through that journey, I learned to love them and loving them means getting out of my comfort zone. It was a whole new learning experience for me and something I thought I would never do, like downloading apps just to keep up with them and looking up for lyrics translations, even learning more about Korean culture because most of their songs have cultural context. As a fan who consumes a lot of what BTS puts out there, it helps me cope with a lot of stress and anxiety on a daily basis.

Among the songs that I listen to that really resonate with me is "Answer: Love Myself," which is a direct note to myself, a reminder that every day I need to choose to love myself despite everything. I also love "Spring Day," the whole message and deep symbolism of it, which are both painful and endearing. For their heavier, more intense songs, "Not Today" and their live stages of it are my most replayed videos on YouTube.

Meanwhile, RM's *Mono* is like a blanket that comforts me when I feel alone. BTS speaks to me in ways that I couldn't imagine a pop group can do. I thought it's not possible, but I'm here in this Bangtan hole forever.

The most memorable moment in my ARMY life was their *Love Yourself* concert in Hong Kong. I thought and expected that I'd cry but I was just left speechless. It was as if I was in a trance after the whole concert because of how surreal everything was. It was surreal to the point that I couldn't even remember some parts of the concert that I had to look at the photos and stories I took. I intentionally didn't record the encore though, as I wanted it buried in my heart. And it was the happiest night of my life.

©Ashley Cruz

©Ashley Cruz

THE INSPIRING RELATIONSHIP OF BTS MEMBERS

Briana Williams, 25, USA

I have been a K-pop fan since 2007 and kept up with new groups as much as I could. In 2014, I studied at Yonsei University in Seoul for a semester. While there, I got the chance to see the *Brave Concert* that was held on campus. BTS performed "Danger" and "Boy in Luv," and I immediately turned to my friend and asked who those seven boys were. I could tell they had a lot of potential and a lot of heart. They only performed two songs since they were really unknown at the time, but they poured their heart and soul into those two performances. Thankfully, my friend was a BTS fan and told me all about them. That same night, we sat on the floor of my dorm watching their music videos, which enabled me to learn about the members. That was five years ago, and I never once regretted watching that performance.

Everyone knows K-pop groups are put together by companies, but one thing that has always stood out to me about BTS is how they came together as seven boys all from very different backgrounds, who clashed, argued, and experienced hardships. But they didn't let differences or difficulties stop them. They figured out their strengths as a group and became each other's family. Not only has BTS shown me how to love myself and how to take time to focus on myself, they've also shown me that you really

©Briana Williams

can make your own family. You can surround yourself with positive people who want the best for you because your success and happiness make them happy. BTS shows us it's okay to express emotions and to deal with them head-on. Their music helped me ground myself in the days when I don't feel like myself. Their lyrics help me feel whole again when I start slipping into a dark place. Not only their words, but their relationship also makes me feel so much better, watching

how they interact and care for each other in their own ways.

"Save Me" is by far one of my all-time favorite BTS songs. When I first heard it, it made me realize how much I needed someone to ground me, and that it was okay to depend on others sometimes. I was going to be okay.

From RM's mixtape *Mono*, "Everythingoes" has touched my heart in a way that no other song has ever done. I cried the first time I listened to it. It has such a simple message: everything will pass. Whatever hardships and struggles you may be facing will all pass one day.

BTS PULLED ME OUT OF A DARK PLACE
Pa Chia V., 25, USA

There's this commonality in ARMYs about how we all found BTS when we needed them the most. Every one of us has a story and this is mine: I found BTS at the time of a friend's passing, when I was lost, desolate, and shaken by the world. Alongside this, I was also harboring a trauma that I experienced at a young age. I grew up in an Asian household and we don't talk about our emotions, so I kept everything inside. It created a very dark place inside of me. I kept a happy facade but inside, I was so sad and I hated myself. But then BTS found me: a lost, scared, hurt, and angry soul and they helped me heal. Their words, their lyrics, their genuineness, their humanity, but most importantly, their love helped me. They gave me the courage to not let my past hurt me but helped me see it as a lesson learned. BTS showed me that I have reasons to love myself just as fiercely as I love them. I've loved them since August 2014 and I will continue to love them until the end of time.

I love BTS for their honesty, humility, passion, friendship, and their willingness to show their human side. They go beyond their music, which has been my comfort, my confidant, my safe zone. You can hear their passion and their unbelievable talent in each and every single song, whether it's a beautiful ballad like "The Truth Untold" or a fun, pop "DNA" or in hidden tracks like "Born Singer." In an unforgiving and harsh industry, BTS has stood the test of time through hard work. They never forget where they came from.

I've listened to K-pop for more than ten years. I've followed groups from Shinhwa, SES, TVXQ, and Girls' Generation, to Ateez and Twice. But there is no one else quite like BTS. In this industry, it is all about embodying an idol: pristine and perfect. But BTS is willing to show the ARMYs everything, from member fights to their fears and tears, as well as mistakes they make on stage.

Because of BTS I'm so much happier, I'm slowing down and enjoying my life. I have a newfound appreciation for the littlest things now, and I've also found my forever friends. I have this incredible community of friends and I know that I'm never alone.

©Pa Chia V.

I love every single BTS song but the three that touched me to my core: "Sea," "Whalien 52," and "Mikrokosmos." I love these songs so much so that I got tattoos inspired by them to always remind me that there's always hope in my trials ("Sea"), that I'm not alone anymore ("Whalien 52"), and that I have a light all of my own ("Mikrokosmos"). BTS are my pride, my love, my "Magic Shop," my forever.

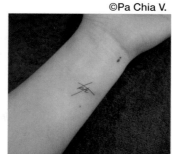

WRITING BTS'S STORY
FROM THE AUTHOR,
DIANNE PINEDA-KIM

After following BTS for years, researching about them for months, reading every news article, re-watching videos, and listening to every song—I'm at a loss of words on how to go about my own BTS story. It's been a rollercoaster ride, writing this book. But let me start first by saying that they came at a time when I was at my lowest point.

I was sitting at home alone in front of my computer wondering what my next step will be after having finished all my writing projects for the past few months. Being a freelance writer and editor meant that there would be times when I'm extremely busy one day and a complete bum in the next. After moving to Korea and quitting my full-time editor job at a publishing company to marry my Korean husband, this has been my usual repertoire. It took a while getting used to it but I still feel grateful to be living without the confines of the corporate world. But that time I purposefully did not accept any work because I knew I wouldn't be able to do it for a couple of months—because of an impending surgery I had to go through.

I had been going back and forth to hospitals because of pain and discomfort in my lower abdomen. Doctors told me it would be hard for me to conceive a baby. My husband and I were devastated.

Fortunately, we found a good hospital in Gangnam, Seoul with a skilled, caring doctor who was willing to perform abdominal myomectomy, a very sensitive procedure to remove multiple benign tumors. I was feeling a mix of emotions: panicked, scared out of my wits yet relieved to hear that I still have a chance. It was right at that moment when I received an email from my publisher, asking if I can write a book about BTS. Me. Book. BTS. All the words looked incoherent to me because my eyes were already filled with tears before I could even finish reading the email.

I have been a fan since their "Dope" era, have already released a K-pop Style book the year prior, and I'm also a features writer for *Soompi* (a Seoul-based K-pop site), and not to mention, being a K-pop fan for years—so surely, I can do it, right? But even though I had said yes in a heartbeat, I immediately started getting anxious and wondered if it was the right decision. I have written about BTS quite a lot of times for *Soompi* but every time, I feel a huge pressure because I know millions of people who love them will have access to it. But writing a book entirely about BTS is a whole other story and I felt a big responsibility put on my shoulders. Plus this book has a word count four times longer than my previous book!

Of course, I always stay true to my journalistic roots to make sure I write objectively and back my articles with research regardless of the topic. But how could I separate myself as a BTS fan, a professional writer, and someone going through difficult personal and health problems while writing this book?

Just a little background story. Even before I got this book project I had been watching a lot of BTS's live streams and keeping updated through Twitter and Weverse. It's hard to choose a favorite song or member, but I found myself "stanning" V for his fashionable looks, artistic sensibilities, and deep, romantic voice. I also adore RM because he is like a voice of reason that keeps on giving great pieces of advice through interviews and songs, whether he intends to or not. But then again, there's J-Hope's infectious cheerfulness (and sometimes silly jokes), Suga's mysterious vibe and "savage" clapbacks, Jimin's magical dances, Jin's unwavering confidence, and Jungkook's mischievous yet adorable personality. Who can choose just one?

Their story of overcoming their humble beginnings and difficulties is truly inspiring. Everybody said they wouldn't make it. Meanwhile several naysayers still doubt their success until now. But their brotherhood, dedication, and passion continue to pay off and they pay it forward by sharing their gift to fans. If you're an ARMY like me and have watched their practice videos, concert preps, busy shoots, and recording sessions, you probably know how hard they work. They always have their game face on, rehearsing nonstop no matter how exhausted they must've felt.

And what's great about them is that they don't seem to have an air of "celebrity" about them; they remain so humble, wholesome, and unaffected by fame, even when caught

©Dianne Pineda-Kim

off cam. You can tell they are genuine, and that's what draws millions of fans toward them. I really think every person can learn something from BTS, even those who are not K-pop fans.

Thinking about this, I decided to let go of my fears both of getting surgery and accepting the task at hand. Fast forward after the surgery, I was in my hospital bed for a week listening to BTS's song "Home."

Every time a nurse came to check in on me, she would catch me watching *Run BTS* episodes, laughing to myself. Their songs "Euphoria," "Magic Shop," "Serendipity," "Answer: Love Myself," and "Mama" helped me get distracted from the pain I felt.

After I got home from the hospital, that's

when I started doing extensive research and, in a way, they were part of my healing process. They were not only a welcome distraction but also comforting friends. Every single day I woke up I read, watched, and wrote about them. And there was not a single time when it felt like work.

This is for all the ARMYs and curious readers of this book. From the outside, I may be one of the authors who wrote about them, but in reality, we wrote their story together. Reading each and every one of my interviews with fans made me realize that the ARMYs add each chapter to their narrative, and the pages keep on growing.

I am afraid that after I finish writing this book I will feel empty, as though the boys who had kept me company all this time will be gone. But one thing's for sure—it was my pleasure to have been part of this book. If there's one thing I learned both from BTS and in life, it's that every person deserves and will always have the chance to heal, to rise above difficulties or failures, to love, and—ultimately—to be happy.

CHAPTER 12

MAKING A BIG DIFFERENCE: BTS INTO THE FUTURE

One of the lines in the lead song "Boy with Luv" on the *Map of the Soul Persona* album, says: "You're the star that turns ordinaries into extraordinaries."

At the end of this road you walk alone
Will you step on it, whatever there may be
Sometimes we may get tired or sick
That's okay, I am by your side
If you and I are together
We can smile

I want to fly though I have no wings
But your hands become my wings
I want to forget the dark and lonely things
Together with you

These wings sprouted from my pain

But these wings are going towards the light
Even if it's tiring and painful, I will fly if I can
Will you hold my hand
So that I won't be afraid anymore?
If you and I are together
I can smile

**— BTS, "A Supplementary Story:
You Never Walk Alone"[159]**

SEVERAL MUSIC INDUSTRY ANALYSTS HAVE sought to find the formula for BTS's success, and although they can help us understand the reasons behind their meteoric rise, there will always be certain factors that cannot be encapsulated as their story has barely begun. Bang Si-hyuk told *Korea JoongAng Daily* in 2017, "It is too early to talk about success, and it is difficult to share any secret to success as of now."

In terms of economic success, however, it is easy to draw from credible sources that have documented the business aspect of their career. *Forbes* proclaimed that BTS is the "World's highest paid boy band and K-Pop act" in its 2019 Celebrity 100 List, where the band debuted at number forty-three, taking home $57 million in gross income over the previous year.[160] The media company reported that "a significant portion of the group's earnings derive from its massive 'Love Yourself World Tour' and its corresponding 'Love Yourself: Speak Yourself' Stadium Tour extension, in support of their record-breaking Love Yourself album trilogy: Her, Tear and Answer. This also included the release of two concert films, 'Burn The Stage: The Movie,' which tallied $18.5 million globally, and 'BTS World Tour: Love Yourself in Seoul,' a concert movie in honor of their world tour; the latter clocked $11.7 million worldwide (excluding Korea) as of January. Endorsement deals with brands like Hyundai and Coca Cola added millions as well."

With whopping sales records that continue to soar with each music, film, product or BTS-related brand release, *Forbes* is anticipating that "the group's prospects bode well for a Celebrity 100 return next year."

Looking at BTS's achievements from a broader perspective, they have not only created a big impact on their company and individual earnings but also on Korea's annual economy. SBS News reported in June 2019 that BTS has added over five trillion Korean Won (approximately 4.6 billion USD) to Korea's economy.[161] Data by Hyundai Research Institute also revealed that BTS was the reason that one in every thirteen foreign tourists visited South Korea in 2017, and according to Yonhap News Agency, it is estimated that over 800,000 tourists come to Korea each year because of the group. The figure is equal to 7.6 percent of 10.4 million foreign tourists who visited the country last year, the institute said.[162]

For this reason, the Korean government has placed high hopes for BTS to carry the country's name in promoting it to the world. In 2018, the band became brand ambassadors for Seoul's tourism campaign, which was dubbed "My Seoul Playlist." It featured each member in a video commercial with his own Seoul playlist centered around a particular theme, showing the capital city's main attractions.

With their undeniably wholesome image and the band's status as one of the world's most influential stars, Korean and global brands—namely, Puma, Converse, Hyundai, Mediheal, Lotte Duty Free, SK Telecom, Fila, and many others—clamored to enlist the group as the faces of their campaigns. BTS represented a variety of Korean brands, including cosmetics, apparel, and food, department stores, telecommunications, and banking.

Their strength does not simply lie on their name extension, packaging, or the product itself: it's in the engagement of consumers online. People are not only buying BTS-stamped products, they talk about it too. What BTS has done is not only create a hype or recall for a brand, they have also been able to initiate conversations about the product they endorse across diverse target markets.

"Out of all the social media engagement we had this year, BTS is number one," said Brian Mariotti, CEO of Funko Inc., an American company that manufactures licensed pop culture collectibles. The company released vinyl figurines of the band. "And that's ahead of 'Game of Thrones,' 'Avengers: Endgame,' and that's a surprise to us and it's a huge win. And we got to see how powerful the BTS brand [is] at New York Toy Fair." Mariotti also mentioned that BTS items were the most talked about topic on their Instagram, Twitter, and Facebook channels.

The group's savvy marketing strategies, social media engagement, and creative content creation all have contributed to their commercial success, but ultimately it is their CEO's clever decision-making and goal of elevating K-pop music that have greatly helped make BTS stand out from the countless K-pop groups debuting and promoting at a rapid pace.

"When I first planned for BTS and proposed the idea and concept, what I actually felt was that the fans from Western culture and Japan caught and understood the storylines really fast. In Korean culture, on the other hand, I felt there was even rejection at first," Bang Si-hyuk said.[163] At the beginning of BTS's career, the CEO got a lot of feedback from Korean audiences asking him to just create cool songs "rather than make them try to understand useless storylines and discuss different theories."

Bang's strategy eventually paid off. In addition to giving their songs a deeper meaning and making the audience participate in understanding stories behind them, BTS was able to bypass the long-established routes that most K-pop groups are accustomed to taking. "Previous generation of K-Pop idols are very much dependent on TV as a platform, whereas BTS used social media to really make themselves available and visible, and that can be done anywhere and around the world. BTS circumvented the traditional model of debuting on TV music shows and gaining visibility by taking a route of reaching fans through social media directly. So it is a band that gained fame and popularity overseas even before they became superstars in Korea itself," Suk-Young Kim, a professor of critical studies at the University of California, Los Angeles, told CNBC.

Breaking through language barriers is another of the biggest accomplishments made by BTS, if not the most astounding. Their songs are primarily in Korean—save for their collaborations with Western artists like Charli XCX, Ed Sheeran, The Chainsmokers, Steve Aoki, Zara Larsson, Halsey, and others—with only the chorus or a few lines in English. In an unprecedented feat, BTS was able to make international artists adjust to their language, and not the other way around.

BTS stayed true to their musical style as well as their native language, proving that music, or good music, rather, knows no limits. "[Whether it's] English or Korean, we have the same message," Suga told Ellen DeGeneres during their appearance on *The Ellen DeGeneres Show*. The same can be said about their concerts, where, according to Jungkook, "Even in concerts abroad, the fans sing along to our songs in Korean. I'm truly grateful for that. It made me want to keep on studying languages without giving up, to be able to express my thoughts in my own words."

In a radio interview, singer Halsey explained how the band is making big strides as a non-English-speaking act just like many successful Latin artists. "It takes time. I think people are starting to come around to the idea of accepting music as a nonverbal expression and there's something that's a little bit more abstract than that, so watching the Latin artists get their break in English-speaking countries gives me hope that artists like BTS is pioneering a path for their music to be more commercial."

Eve Tan, Singapore-based team leader for Asian content at Spotify, has also recognized this unique achievement not just by BTS but K-pop in general. "For a genre that is in a different language and from a very different culture, it is very inspiring to see how K-pop is making its mark on the global stage."[164]

I don't have biceps or pecs
I don't have a super car like Batman
The ideal hero is my fantasy
But all I can give you is Anpan
I've dreamed of becoming a hero like Superman
I ran with all my strength, jumping high up
   in the sky
I'm not afraid of little things like bruising
   my knees
Innocent fantasies of my childhood

I'm not a superhero
Don't expect a lot
I can be your hero
                    — BTS, "Anpanman"[165]

In the song "Anpanman," a name inspired by a cartoon character, BTS sang about wanting to protect and give strength to people even though they're not real superheroes. ARMYs have found this to be true as they were comforted, inspired, and motivated by their songs, which resonated with a lot of people.

"Our lyrics deal with real issues that face all humans: choices in life, depression, self-esteem," RM told *Time*. Their message is not just a one-way street. BTS members themselves have admitted to experiencing these hardships, and they share these as well as the ARMYs' stories through their songs. "ARMYs tell us about their feelings, failures, passions, and struggles all the time," RM added. "We are often inspired by them, because we try to write about how real young people—like the seven of us—face real-life issues. Most of our music is about how we perceive the world and how we try to persist as normal, average human beings. So our fans inspire us and give us a direction to go as musicians."

While music is first and foremost what BTS wants to get recognized for, their good looks and fashion are inextricably linked to their presentation as a whole. Their stage wardrobe consists of a variety of gender-bending styles and silhouettes, such as frilly shirts, furs, touches of pink, sequins, and bold prints, complemented by colorful hairstyles and makeup looks that are not uncommon for most K-pop stars. They often deviate from the distinctive, sporty, big fashion styles that hip-hop and rap artists

are known to wear. Their courage to sing about social issues is tantamount to how they confidently embrace a variety of styles and stick to them even at the risk of being criticized.

This adds to their unique charm, as Grammy.com notes, "They defy gender norms and push aside outdated ideas of pop star masculinity via their fashion and music choices."

"BTS have changed the perception in a way that people love these boys who change their hair colors all the times and wear makeup," New York-based music journalist Jeff Benjamin told the *Korea Times*.[166] "I think this is awesome because people respond to them not only for their music and visuals,

but also find them attractive and beautiful. It seems they are changing some stereotypes about Korean males and the idea of what an attractive man is."

"The effect was a welcome disruption of what we expect a male heartthrob to look and sound like—a radical cultural act made only more encouraging by how enthusiastically it was received by the diverse crowd inside Staples Center," wrote pop music critic Mikael Wood for *Chicago Tribune.*[167]

In the same way that they help widen the perception of male attractiveness, they also factor into the conversation about diversity and representation. Speaking about his collaboration with BTS for the song "Waste It on Me," which featured Asian actors instead of the BTS members, Steve Aoki said, "It's bigger than music, it represents a Korean band and an Asian-American DJ that can show other Asians that they're also a part of the global musical landscape. I feel so deeply about the Asian footprint in music culture, I wanted the music video to have entire Asian cast and director."

BTS, however, do not think of themselves as a trailblazing boy band that took the music world by storm. "We are standing here thanks to the road laid by many artists who came before us," Jin said at a press conference.

"I'd be lying if I said BTS never felt any pressure. I'm feeling the pressure now. We do feel pressure. So we commit ourselves to carrying on our work."

More than pressure, BTS found themselves taking on bigger responsibilities beyond their music. In 2017, BTS launched "Love Myself," an anti-violence campaign developed with the United Nations Children's Fund (UNICEF), to spread awareness against violence toward children and teens around the world. The campaign's central message is: "True love first begins with loving myself."

The effort was promoted with the help of the hashtags #EndViolence and #BTSLoveMyself, which asked fans and supporters to post photos showing positivity to different social media platforms. As of April 2019, the accumulated funds BTS was able to raise according to the official website is 2.4 billion Korean Won, almost two million dollars. The hashtag has been used all over the world over ten million times.[168]

In September 2018, BTS joined United Nations members, international representatives of global businesses, young people, and education leaders at the launch of Generation Unlimited in New York at the seventy-third session of the UN General Assembly. RM gave a powerful speech with the other BTS members standing behind him.

BTS Members attended a UNICEF campaign meeting at the UN headquarters on September 24, 2018 in New York City. Here is an excerpt:

My name is Kim Nam Joon, also known as RM, the leader of the group BTS. It's an incredible honour to be invited to an occasion with such significance for today's young generation. I would like to begin by talking about myself.

I was born in Ilsan, a city near Seoul, South Korea. It's a beautiful place, with a lake, hills, and even an annual flower festival. I spent a happy childhood there, and I was just an ordinary boy.

I would look up at the night sky in wonder and dream the dreams of a boy. I used to imagine that I was a superhero, saving the world.

In an intro to one of our early albums, there is a line that says, "My heart stopped . . . I was maybe nine or ten."

Looking back, that's when I began to worry about what other people thought of me and started seeing myself through their eyes. I stopped looking up at the stars at night. I stopped daydreaming. I tried to jam myself into moulds that other people made. Soon, I began to shut out my own voice and started to listen to the voices of others. No one called out my name, and neither did I. My heart stopped and my eyes closed shut. So, like this, I, we, all lost our names. We became like ghosts.

I had one sanctuary, and that was music. There was a small voice in me that said, "Wake up, man, and listen to yourself!" Even after making the decision to join BTS, there were hurdles. Most people thought we were hopeless. Sometimes, I just wanted to quit.

I think I was very lucky that I didn't give it all up.

I'm sure that I, and we, will keep stumbling and falling. We have become artists performing in huge stadiums and selling millions of albums.

But I am still an ordinary, twenty-four-year-old guy. If there's anything that I've achieved, it was only possible because I had my other BTS members by my side, and because of the love and support of our ARMY fans.

Maybe I made a mistake yesterday, but yesterday's me is still me. I am who I am today, with all my faults. Tomorrow I might be a tiny bit wiser, and that's me, too. These faults and mistakes are what I am, making up the brightest stars in the constellation of my life. I have come to love myself for who I was, who I am, and who I hope to become.

After releasing the *Love Yourself* albums and launching the "Love Myself" campaign, we started to hear remarkable stories from our fans all over the world, how our message helped them overcome their hardships in life and start loving themselves. These stories constantly remind us of our responsibility.

So, let's all take one more step. We have learned to love ourselves, so now I urge you to "speak yourself." Tell me your story. I want to hear your voice, and I want to hear your conviction. No matter who you are, where you're from, your skin colour, gender identity: speak yourself.[169]

Aside from publicly disclosed social responsibility campaigns, the members themselves have secretly given donations to charitable institutions. Member Jin has donated more than 100 million won (around $88,000 in US dollars) to UNICEF, becoming a member of Korea Honors Club, a club for sponsors who donated a cumulative sum of 100 million won. He later decided not to announce publicly that he had made the donation and remained silent for over a year but agreed to reveal that he had joined the Honors Club, in hopes of spreading awareness and urging people to donate as well.[170]

When he turned twenty-six, Suga donated $90,000 to a nonprofit foundation that supports child cancer patients, according to Korea Paediatric Cancer Foundation. He also gave more than 300 dolls he designed as a gift to the patients. It was not the first time he made donations.[171] According to a report by *Soompi*, Jimin donated 100 million won (approximately $87,914) to Busan Metropolitan City Office of Education to be used toward education development. The other members have also participated in philanthropic efforts, which in turn inspired the ARMYs to follow suit. Fans have donated a total of 30 million won (approximately $26,373) to the Hope Bridge Korea Disaster Relief Association in the name of BTS to help the victims of Gangwon Province wildfire.[172]

"That makes us think more about our responsibilities, how we should act, how we should make our music. So it makes us think more deeply about what we do, how responsible we should be about what we're doing, and the music we're making," Jungkook shared via a translator in an interview at the Grammy Museum.[173]

Since 2013, BTS hasn't had an extended break. In August 2019, Big Hit Entertainment announced that the group would be taking a much-needed hiatus for two months to focus on rest and relaxation, seeing it as an "opportunity for the members of BTS, who have relentlessly driven themselves towards their goal since their debut, to recharge and present themselves anew as musicians and creators. This will also provide them with a chance to enjoy the ordinary lives of young people in their 20s, albeit briefly."

Fans responded positively to the announcement, and just after BTS came back from their short break, Bang Si-hyuk revealed at a press conference that he has big plans for the group. "We are working with a famous Korean drama production company to produce a drama where the theme is based off of BTS's outlook of the world, which is expected to be revealed in the second half of 2020. We are also preparing a new game with Netmarble using BTS's storytelling IP (intellectual property)."

"BTS have relentlessly driven themselves toward their goal since their debut," a statement from their company read.

ABOUT THE AUTHOR

DIANNE PINEDA-KIM IS AN EDITOR FOR VARIOUS PRINT MAGAZINES AND WEBSITES IN South Korea. She writes about K-pop fashion trends and entertainment features for Soompi.com, a division of Viki Inc., the world's largest and longest-running English online medium, providing complete coverage of Korean pop culture. She is also a fashion editor for Groove Korea, a Seoul-based magazine that publishes guides and features for expats living in Korea. She has done coverage on Seoul Fashion Week for CNN Style, an architect feature for Chicago-based design magazine *Sixtysix*, and several other works for international media. She has published a book titled *K-Pop Style: Fashion, Skin Care, Makeup, Lifestyle, and More* for Skyhorse Publishing, Inc. She is a BTS ARMY for life. Follow her personal Instagram at @dianne_panda and travel guide account @iwonderkorea.

REFERENCES

Chapter 1

1. Time. (2018, June 28). *Rap Monster of Breakout K-Pop Band BTS on Fans, Fame and Viral Popularity*. Retrieved from https://time.com/4833807/rap-monster-bts-interview/
2. CNBC. (2019, July 10). *How BTS Became A Major Moneymaker For South Korea.* Retrieved from https://www.youtube.com/watch?v=vpNIwap2YoQ&feature=share&fbclid=IwAR-1jnCpAOc5Z-7VdYEeNJxkuyQlcMc_pgXO75NSt2aIBsoSs27v14QikkQU
3. Nikki Lab. (2019, June 30). *Meet 10 Enthusiastic BTS ARMYs at Seoul MUSTER.* Retrieved from https://www.youtube.com/watch?v=rWaKFzxds5k&fbclid=IwAR3-YNIFvORW8IuTgjd-CwnkAdAM-jsSF5UTTavWIPVmxoiePE5pJIO-Isxs

Chapter 2

4. AllKpop. (2017, July 5). *BTS now stands for "Beyond The Scene."* Retrieved from https://www.allkpop.com/article/2017/07/bts-now-stands-for-beyond-the-scene
5. Vox. (2019, April 17). *BTS, the band that changed K-pop, explained.* https://www.vox.com/culture/2018/6/13/17426350/bts-history-members-explained.
6. Billboard Chart FAQ. Retrieved from https://www.billboard.com/p/faq
7. Soompi. (2018, May 28). *BTS Makes History As "Love Yourself: Tear" Enters Billboard 200 At No.1.* Retrieved from https://www.soompi.com/article/1176577wpp/bts-makes-history-love-tear-enters-billboard-200-incredible-ranking
8. Korea Herald. (2019, April 22). *BTS becomes 1st band since Beatles to score 3 Billboard No. 1 albums in single year*. Retrieved from http://www.koreaherald.com/view.php?ud=20190422000117
9. Soompi. (2019, August 24). *BTS Achieves 2nd Gold Album In U.S. After "Map Of The Soul: Persona" Earns RIAA Certification.* Retrieved from https://www.soompi.com/article/1347710wpp/bts-achieves-2nd-gold-album-in-u-s-after-map-of-the-soul-perso-na-earns-riaa-certification?fbclid=IwAR2MntV5Wrbt2jz2uXv5qFu-KOVf99TY124u6BU4jx-K9mSpf6rWqYNqHNUg
10. Forbes. (January 24, 2020). *BTS is the First Korean Act to Earn an RIAA Platinum Album Certification*. Retrieved from https://www.forbes.com/sites/bryanrolli/2020/01/24/bts-is-the-first-korean-act-to-earn-an-riaa-platinum-album-certification/#74db0ecd2153
11. Billboard Chart History. Retrieved from https://www.billboard.com/music/bts/chart-history/billboard-200
12. Official Charts. (2019, April 15). *BTS set for their first Number 1 on the UK's Official Albums Chart with Map of the Soul: Persona*. Retrieved from https://www.officialcharts.com/chart-news/bts-set-for-their-first-number-1-on-the-u-k-s-official-albums-chart-with-map-of-the-soul-persona__26072/
13. Billboard. (2020, January 15). *BTS Has Already Sold *How* Many Albums? Label Reveals Massive 'Map of the Soul: 7' Pre-Orders*. Retrieved from https://www.billboard.com/articles/news/bts/8548179/bts-map-of-the-soul-7-pre-orders

14. Forbes. (2020, February 18). *BTS's 'Map of the Soul: 7' Is Now the Most Preordered South Korean Album of All Time.* https://www.forbes.com/sites/hughmcintyre/2020/02/18/btss-map-of-the-soul-7-is-now-the-most-preordered-south-korean-album-of-all-time/#675151a673de

15. Soompi. (2020, January 18). *BTS Breaks Record As "Black Swan" Soars To Top Of iTunes Charts All Over The World*. Retrieved from https://www.soompi.com/article/1377716wpp/bts-breaks-record-as-black-swan-soars-to-top-of-itunes-charts-all-over-the-world

16. Naver Entertainment. (2017, December 24). *BTS, 13th place on the Oricon Chart, Top ranking among K-pop singers*. Retrieved from https://entertain.naver.com/now/read?oid=011&aid=0003181643

17. iHeartRadio. (2018, September 20). *15 Times BTS Broke Huge Records*. Retrieved from https://www.iheart.com/content/2018-09-20-15-times-bts-broke-huge-records/

18. Soompi. (2018, May 25). *BTS Breaks Record With 1 Million Albums Sold In 1st Week.* Retrieved from https://www.soompi.com/article/1175313wpp/bts-breaks-record-1-million-albums-sold-1st-week

19. Nielsen Music Mid-Year Report US 2019. Retrieved from https://www.nielsen.com/wp-content/uploads/sites/3/2019/06/nielsen-us-music-mid-year-report-2019.pdf?wgu=11671_16644_15765547409999_45ece38651&wgexpiry=1584330740&afflt=ntrt15490001&afflt_uid=11671_16644_15765547409999_45ece38651&afflt_uid_2=AFFLT_ID_2

20. Time. (2018, October 10). *How BTS Is Taking Over the World*. Retrieved from https://time.com/collection-post/5414052/bts-next-generation-leaders/

21. Grammy. (2019, February 22). *K-Pop Phenoms BTS Keep Breaking Records: Here's Why*. Retrieved from https://www.grammy.com/grammys/news/k-pop-phenoms-bts-keep-breaking-records-heres-why

Chapter 3

22. Lyrics Translate. (2019, July, 3). *Lights*. Retrieved from https://lyricstranslate.com/en/lights-lights.html-0

23. English translation credit: @kookceptional on Twitter. Permanent Twitter user ID: 953273548780351489. https://twitter.com/kookceptional

24. The Telegraph. (2019, June 3). *The Korean Beatles: how BTS are changing the language of pop*. Retrieved from https://www.telegraph.co.uk/music/artists/behind-scenes-bts-korean-beatles-defy-boy-band-tradition-demand/amp/?__twitter_impression=true&fbclid=IwAR3OhL2He2jcZcMKfgWd4cptQp8QJFrTFaXXgxYylNvm1kKQNEOMKHitPlA

25. Guiness World Records. *Most Twitter engagements (average retweets).* Retrieved from https://www.guinnessworldrecords.com/world-records/471737-most-twitter-engagements-tweet-interactions

26. The Telegraph. (2018, October 16). *Inside ARMY: The bizarre and beautiful world of BTS fandom*. Retrieved from https://www.telegraph.co.uk/music/artists/inside-army-bizarre-beautiful-world-bts-fandom/

27. Billboard. (2019, April 12). *BTS First Asian Act to Surpass 5 Billion Streams on Spotify*. Retrieved from https://www.billboard.com/articles/news/bts/8506971/bts-first-asian-kpop-artist-5-billion-streams-spotify

28. AllKpop. (2017, August 23). *ARMYs are asking American retailer 'Target' to start shelving BTS albums.* Retrieved from https://www.allkpop.com/article/2017/08/armys-are-asking-american-retailer-target-to-start-shelving-bts-albums

29. Grammy. (2019, May 16). *BTS Shine At GRAMMY U SoundChecks In Chicago*. Retrieved from https://www.grammy.com/membership/news/bts-shine-grammy-u-soundchecks-chicago?amp&__twitter_impression=true&fbclid=IwAR18MQs2ufKdjcDZf12jNdqVWGwPTFar-WR2R2Fe9anDrQXeAPiT_SSizYck

Chapter 4

30. English translation credit: @kookceptional on Twitter. Permanent Twitter user ID: 953273548780351489. https://twitter.com/kookceptional
31. The Korea Times. (2019, June 16). *BTS rakes in record-breaking $79 million from stadium tour.* Retrieved from http://www.koreatimes.co.kr/www/art/2019/06/682_270890.html
32. The Telegraph. (2018, October 16). *Inside ARMY: The bizarre and beautiful world of BTS fandom.* Retrieved from https://www.telegraph.co.uk/music/artists/inside-army-bizarre-beautiful-world-bts-fandom/
33. The Korea Herald. (2019, June 2). *BTS performs at historic sold-out Wembley concert.* Retrieved from http://www.koreaherald.com/view.php?ud=20190602000198

Chapter 5

34. Genius. *Idol.* Retrieved from https://genius.com/Genius-english-translations-bts-idol-english-translation-lyrics
35. Korea Herald. (2017, November 2). *More than half of foreigners visit Korea after watching hallyu content: poll.* Retrieved from http://www.koreaherald.com/view.php?ud=20171102000169&ACE_SEARCH=1
36. Korea Herald. (2019, May 3). *Hallyu gains steam with exports rising 9.1% in 2018.* Retrieved from http://www.koreaherald.com/view.php?ud=20190503000437
37. The Korea Times. (2015, January 27). *Confucianism is cultural genes of Koreans.* Retrieved from http://www.koreatimes.co.kr/www/news/culture/2015/01/148_172505.html
38. CEFIA. *Korean Confucianism - 4. Self-Cultivation: The Way of Learning to be Human.* Retrieved from http://cefia.aks.ac.kr:84/index.php?title=Korean_Confucianism_-_4._Self-Cultivation:_The_Way_of_Learning_to_be_Human
39. BBC. (2016, January 26). *The dark side of Asia's pop music industry.* Retrieved from https://www.bbc.com/news/world-asia-35368705
40. Asian Boss. *Confessions Of A Former K-pop Idol (ft. Crayon Pop).* Retrieved from https://www.youtube.com/watch?time_continue=393&v=KdOA5BCwBi0
41. SBS. (2017, December 14). *The dark side of K-pop (according to a former K-pop idol).* Retrieved from https://www.sbs.com.au/popasia/blog/2017/12/14/dark-side-k-pop-according-former-k-pop-idol

Chapter 6

42. YouTube. (2018, February 23). *BTS and Bang PD nim Preview for Good Insight.* Retrieved from https://www.youtube.com/watch?v=ETlu1QA5flk
43. Channel Korea. (2019, April 26). *Meet the mastermind behind BTS' hit songs, "Hitman Bang Shi Hyuk!"* Retrieved from https://channel-korea.com/hitman-bang-bang-shi-hyuk-profile/
44. The Korea Herald. (2019, February 17). *Big Hit CEO Bang Si-hyuk says 'anger is driving force' at SNU commencement.* Retrieved from http://kpopherald.koreaherald.com/view.php?ud=20190227175057974162_2
45. CNBC. (2019, July 10). *How BTS Became A Major Moneymaker For South Korea.* Retrieved from https://www.youtube.com/watch?v=vpNlwap2YoQ&feature=share&fbclid=IwAR-1jnCpAOc5Z-7VdYEeNJxkuyQlcMc_pgXO75NSt2alBsoSs27v14QikkQU
46. Soompi. (2018, January 7). *Bang Shi Hyuk Shares The Secret To BTS's Success And His Ultimate Goal For The Group.* Retrieved from https://www.soompi.com/article/1104305wpp/bang-shi-hyuk-shares-secret-btss-success-ultimate-goal-group
47. Grammy Awards. (2019, February 22). *K-Pop Phenoms BTS Keep Breaking Records: Here's Why.* https://www.grammy.com/grammys/news/k-pop-phenoms-bts-keep-breaking-records-heres-why

Chapter 7

48. Genius. *Mikrokosmos*. Retrieved from https://genius.com/
Genius-english-translations-bts-mikrokosmos-english-translation-lyrics

49. Genius. *Moonchild*. Retrieved from https://genius.com/
Genius-english-translations-rm-moonchild-english-translation-lyrics

50. MNews. (2018, January 4). *A MUST READ: BTS' Boss Tells the Beginning of the Legend That is BTS*. Retrieved from https://mnews.joins.com/
article/22258745?IgnoreUserAgent=y#home

51. ET Online. (2017, November 16). *BTS Answers Fans' Biggest Burning Questions—And RM Reveals Why He Changed His Name From Rap Monster!* Retrieved from https://www.eton-line.com/bts-answers-fans-biggest-burning-questions-and-rm-reveals-why-he-changed-his-name-rap-monster-91173

52. BTS Wiki. Retrieved from https://bts.fandom.com/wiki/RM

53. Soompi. (2017, September 9). *Sleepy Talks About BTS's Rap Monster Before Debut, Tells Story About Meetup With Jin (Featuring Jimin).* Retrieved from https://www.soompi.com/article/1040757wpp/
sleepy-talks-btss-rap-monster-debut-tells-story-meetup-jin-featuring-jimin

54. *Hyung* is the Korean word for "older brother."

55. Genius. *Bulletproof Pt.2*. Retrieved from https://genius.com/
Genius-english-translations-bts-we-are-bulletproof-pt2-english-translation-lyrics

56. Soompi. (2017, October 27). *8 Book Recommendations By BTS's RM That You Won't Be Able To Put Down*. Retrieved from https://www.soompi.com/
article/1061029wpp/8-rap-monster-book-recs

57. SBS. (2018, September 12). *BTS RM's wise words to add to your life philosophy*. Retrieved from https://www.sbs.com.au/popasia/blog/2018/09/12/
bts-rms-wise-words-add-your-life-philosophy

58. Soompi. (2018, November 9). *8 Times BTS's RM Shared Valuable Pieces Of Wisdom*. Retrieved from https://www.soompi.com/
article/1258945wpp/8-times-btss-rm-shared-valuable-pieces-wisdom

59. Genius. *Do You*. Retrieved from https://genius.com/
Genius-english-translations-rm-do-you-english-translation-lyrics

60. DJ Booth. (2019, July 18). *At 24, BTS' RM Is a K-Pop Icon—and Hip-Hop Legend*. Retrieved from https://djbooth.net/features/2019-07-18-bts-rm-hip-hop-legend-kpop-boy-band?fbclid=IwAR1-Q15K7xFKxsxV38DGu-WoXrRvmN-VrzvfGCRoKSAgdMR3PxnSM-jWXJtw

61. NME. *RM, Mono Review*. (2018, October 23). Retrieved from https://www.nme.com/
reviews/album/rm-mono-review#cDimAFHMwjbwDuXj.99

62. Genius. *Uhgood*. Retrieved from https://genius.com/
Genius-english-translations-rm-uhgood-english-translation-lyrics

63. Genius. *Agust D*. Retrieved from https://genius.com/
Genius-english-translations-agust-d-agust-d-english-translation-lyrics

64. Wattpad. *BTS Wings Concept Book Interview: Suga*. https://www.wattpad.com/445020102-bts-wings-concept-book-eng-%E2%9D%9D-interview-suga-%E2%9D%9E/
page/2

65. Billboard. (2016, August 16). *BTS' Suga Addresses Depression & Cost of Fame on 'Agust D' Mixtape*. Retrieved from https://www.billboard.com/articles/columns/k-town/7476080/
bts-suga-agust-d-mixtape

66. Genius. *The Last*. Retrieved from https://genius.com/
Genius-english-translations-agust-d-the-last-english-translation-lyrics

67. Ka Leo. *Agust D Album Review*. (2018, March 3). Retrieved from http://www.manoanow. org/kaleo/features/entertainment/agust-d-album-review/article_6dee9708-1f0f-11e8-870e-639a29abb28a.html

68. Soompi. (2018, April 21). *BTS' Suga, Simon Dominic, Oh Hyuk, And More Chosen To Become Full Members Of Korea Music Copyright Association*. Retrieved from https://www. soompi.com/article/1158185wpp/bts-suga-simon-dominic-oh-hyuk-recognized-korea-music-copyright-association-full-members

69. Genius. *Airplane*. Retrieved from https://genius.com/ Genius-english-translations-j-hope-airplane-english-translation-lyrics

70. Genius. *Road/Path*. Retrieved from https://genius.com/ Genius-english-translations-bts-hidden-track-road-path-english-translation-lyrics

71. TIME. (2018, March 2). *J-hope of K-Pop Sensation BTS Has His Own Story to Tell on New Solo Mixtape*. Retrieved from https://time.com/5181183/j-hope-bts-hope-world-interview/

72. Genius. *Hope World*. Retrieved from https://genius.com/ Genius-english-translations-j-hope-hope-world-english-translation-lyrics

73. Vocal. *Hope World: Album Review*. Retrieved from https://vocal.media/beat/ hope-world-album-review

74. Genius. *Epiphany*. Retrieved from https://genius.com/ Genius-english-translations-bts-epiphany-english-translation-lyrics

75. CZDOLLIC. *Kim Seokjin From South Korea is Number 1 Sculpted face in The World*. Retrieved from https://czdollic.proweb.cz/ kim-seokjin-from-south-korea-is-number-1-sculpted-face-in-the-world

76. The Korea Times. (2019, January 27). *BTS member Jin has world's 'best-sculpted' face*. Retrieved from https://m.koreatimes.co.kr/pages/article.asp?newsIdx=262744

77. K-Pop Herald. (2019, February 15). *50 facts about Jin of BTS*. Retrieved from http:// kpopherald.koreaherald.com/view.php?ud=201902151626099126919_2

78. Stylecaster. (2019, April). *BTS's 7 Members Were Discovered in the Most Unconventional Ways*. Retrieved from https://stylecaster.com/how-bts-members-discovered/

79. Genius. *This night*. Retrieved from https://genius.com/ Genius-english-translations-jin-bts-this-night-english-translation-lyrics

80. English translation credit: @kookceptional on Twitter. Permanent Twitter user ID: 953273548780351489. https://twitter.com/kookceptional/status/1146095091544514560

81. Genius. *We are Bulletproof Pt. 2*. Retrieved from https://genius.com/ Genius-english-translations-bts-we-are-bulletproof-pt2-english-translation-lyrics

82. Wattpad. *BTS Wings Concept Book Interview: Jungkook*. https://www.wattpad. com/445024335-bts-wings-concept-book-eng-%E2%9D%9D-interview-jungkook-%E2%9D%9E

83. Genius. *Road/Path*. Retrieved from https://genius.com/ Genius-english-translations-bts-hidden-track-road-path-english-translation-lyrics

84. Genius. *Begin*. Retrieved from https://genius.com/ Genius-english-translations-bts-begin-english-translation-lyrics

85. SBS. (2019, July 19). *7 times BTS' Jungkook caused a product to sell out*. Retrieved from https://www.sbs.com.au/popasia/blog/2019/07/19/7-times-bts-jungkook-caused-product-sell-out?fbclid=IwAR0x8flvqKSsKpBwyncMPkRUMFnU0BfF1pej1ZTL84-EIIBvKr1I-jAV90Sc

86. AllKpop. (2019, June 24). *Jungkook wins 'Instagrammer Global' title at the MTV Millennial Awards... without having an Instagram account!* Retrieved from https://www.allkpop. com/article/2019/06/jungkook-wins-instagrammer-global-title-at-the-mtv-millennial-awards-without-having-an-instagram-account

87. AllKpop. (2019, July 25). *BTS' Jungkook is the most searched K-Pop idol on YouTube*. Retrieved from https://www.allkpop.com/article/2019/07/bts-jungkook-is-the-most-searched-k-pop-idol-on-youtube?fbclid=IwAR3WzsAf3vi4lbD3NXIyca4UBG7C1qYMNTQDH-QII2K3B-64dEHMGfspGRy8

88. Genius. *Singularity*. Retrieved from https://genius.com/Genius-english-translations-bts-intro-singularity-english-translation-lyrics

89. D Magazine. (2018, October 16). *How BTS, the World's Most Popular Boy Band, Bought a Dallas Artist's Paintings*. Retrieved from https://www.dmagazine.com/arts-entertainment/2018/10/how-bts-the-worlds-most-popular-boy-band-bought-a-dallas-artists-paintings/

90. English translation credit: @kookceptional on Twitter. Permanent Twitter user ID: 953273548780351489. https://twitter.com/kookceptional/status/1146085837114712069

91. Genius. *It's definitely you*. Retrieved from https://genius.com/Genius-english-translations-v-and-jin-its-definitely-you-english-translation-lyricshttps://genius.com/Genius-english-translations-v-and-jin-its-definitely-you-english-translation-lyrics

92. Billboard. (2017, June 30). *Get to know BTS: V*. Retrieved from https://www.billboard.com/articles/columns/k-town/7850225/bts-v-get-to-know

93. Wattpad. *BTS Wings Concept Book Interview: V*. Retrieved from https://www.wattpad.com/445024106-bts-wings-concept-book-eng-%E2%9D%9D-interview-v-%E2%9D%9E

94. Genius. *Intro: Serendipity*. Retrieved from https://genius.com/Genius-english-translations-bts-intro-serendipity-english-translation-lyrics

95. Wattpad. *BTS Wings Concept Book Interview: Jimin*. Retrieved from https://www.wattpad.com/445023965-bts-wings-concept-book-eng-%E2%9D%9D-interview-jimin-%E2%9D%9E

96. AllKpop. (2019, July 27). *BTS Jimin is emerging as a hot symbol of art from France, England to Korea*. Retrieved from https://www.allkpop.com/article/2019/07/bts-jimin-is-emerging-as-a-hot-symbol-of-art-from-france-england-to-korea?fbclid=IwAR29PPGSxEjtbn-VWSR5JcVgFhu1CiOMpGNHah-VA6GJXUk7xnWagq0Pe1Ns

97. Genius. *Lost*. Retrieved from https://genius.com/Genius-english-translations-bts-lost-english-translation-lyrics

98. English translation credit: @kookceptional on Twitter. Permanent Twitter user ID: 953273548780351489. https://twitter.com/kookceptional

99. BTS WIKI. *Jimin*. Retrieved from https://bts.fandom.com/wiki/Jimin

100. Exile Magazine. (2018, March 27). *BTS' J-Hope & Jimin at EXILE Magazine.* Retrieved from https://btsdiary.com/2018/03/27/picturepreview-trans-bts-j-hope-jimin-at-exile-magazine-may-2018-issue-180327/

Chapter 8

101. Genius. *On the Start Line*. Retrieved from https://genius.com/Genius-english-translations-bts-hidden-track-skit-on-the-start-line-english-translation-lyrics

102. Koreaboo. (2018, October 10). *Most F*cked Up Things Antis Ever Did To BTS*. Retrieved from https://www.koreaboo.com/lists/fcked-things-antis-ever-bts-1/

103. AllKpop. (2016, May 7). *Anti-fans plan Twitter attack against BTS + ARMY respond*. Retrieved from https://www.allkpop.com/article/2016/05/anti-fans-plan-twitter-attack-against-bts-army-respond

104. Billboard. *U.S. Authorities Investigate Anonymous Death Threats Against BTS' Jimin Ahead of Upcoming Concerts*. Retrieved from https://www.billboard.com/articles/columns/k-town/8465463/bts-jimin-death-threats-love-yourself-tour-usa

105. Genius. *Airplane Pt. 2*. Retrieved from https://genius.com/Genius-english-translations-bts-airplane-pt2-english-translation-lyrics

106. The Korea Times. (2019, July 7). *Rapper rueful about past careless remarks about BTS*. Retrieved from http://www.koreatimes.co.kr/www/nation/2019/07/682_272317.html

107. The Korea Times. (2019, July 7). *Rapper rueful about past careless remarks about BTS*. Retrieved from http://www.koreatimes.co.kr/www/nation/2019/07/682_272317.html

108. Genius. *Give it to me*. Retrieved from https://genius.com/Genius-english-translations-agust-d-give-it-to-me-english-translation-lyrics

109. Lyrics Translate. (2018, November 30). *Born singer*. Retrieved from https://lyricstranslate.com/en/%D0%B2orn-singer-born-singer.html-0

110. Korea JoongAng Daily. (2019, August 2). *Researcher reveals BTS' global success is down to its ARMY*. Retrieved from http://koreajoongangdaily.joins.com/news/article/article.aspx?aid=3066245&fbclid=IwAR2GVooH5D2pPlNf9t2Z5AqPshRRdFcp-WfYUHBvmKy-KeZJ0j-qN0YzkUG4

Chapter 9

111. Variety. (2019, May 12). *Concert Review: BTS Warm Up Chilly Chicago Night With Sold-Out Stadium Show*. Retrieved from https://variety.com/2019/music/news/concert-review-bts-warm-up-a-chilly-chicago-night-with-sold-out-stadium-show-1203212218/

112. Medium. (2019, April 29). *The Curious Case Of BTS: How Journalism Mistakes Production For Manufacture*. Retrieved from https://medium.com/@selizabethcraven/the-curious-case-of-bts-how-journalism-mistakes-production-for-manufacture-73721c270088

113. Hypable. (2019, April 25). *RM has already proven how much work BTS put into 'Map of the Soul: Persona.'* Retrieved from https://www.hypable.com/rm-has-already-proven-how-much-work-bts-put-into-map-of-the-soul-persona/?fbclid=IwAR1ycnX9iqXywN-OhXF9gqPCOHAubgSxdwrs3EybZ9843gCKtd_zrYpWH4Kc

114. Billboard. (2017, October 2). *BTS's Creative Team Discusses Group's Artistic Narrative*. Retrieved from https://www.billboard.com/articles/columns/k-town/7981991/bts-creative-big-hit-entertainment-interview

115. Genius. *No More Dream*. Retrieved from https://genius.com/Genius-english-translations-bts-no-more-dream-english-translation-lyrics

116. Seventeen. (2019, September 5). *20 Best BTS Quotes That Will Make You Love the Bangtan Boys So Much*. Retrieved from https://www.seventeen.com/celebrity/music/a28928893/best-bts-quotes/

117. Genius. *N.O.* Retrieved from https://genius.com/Genius-english-translations-bts-no-english-translation-lyrics

118. NPR. (2015, April 15). *The All-Work, No-Play Culture Of South Korean Education*. Retrieved from https://www.npr.org/sections/parallels/2015/04/15/393939759/the-all-work-no-play-culture-of-south-korean-education

119. Genius. *I Need U*. Retrieved from https://genius.com/Genius-english-translations-bts-i-need-u-english-translation-lyrics

120. Genius. *Run*. Retrieved from https://genius.com/Genius-english-translations-bts-run-english-translation-lyrics

121. Webtoons. *Save Me*. Retrieved from https://www.webtoons.com/en/drama/bts-save-me/list?title_no=1514&page=1

122. The Bangtan Theory. *BTS INU, Prologue and Run: Retakes on innocence, lost and hardships of growing up*. Retrieved from https://thebangtantheory.wordpress.com/

123. Genius. *Dope*. Retrieved from https://genius.com/Genius-english-translations-bts-dope-english-translation-lyrics

124. The Republic of Korea: Cheong Wa Dae. (2017, June 12). *Address by President Moon Jae-in at the National Assembly Proposing a Government Supplementary Budget*. Retrieved from https://english1.president.go.kr/BriefingSpeeches/Economy/2

125. Financial Times. (2019, February 13). *South Korea unemployment rises to 9-year high*. Retrieved from https://www.ft.com/content/01b3c892-2f1c-11e9-8744-e7016697f225

126. Billboard. (2018, February 18). *BTS Speaks Out In Seoul: The K-Pop Megastars Get Candid About Representing a New Generation*. Retrieved from https://www.billboard.com/articles/news/bts/8099577/bts-interview-billboard-cover-story-2018

127. Soompi. (2017, September 18). *Suga Talks About How BTS Songs Address Social Issues*. Retrieved from https://www.soompi.com/article/1045527wpp/suga-talks-bts-songs-address-social-issues

128. Genius. *Go Go*. Retrieved from https://genius.com/Genius-english-translations-bts-go-go-go-english-translation-lyrics

129. Culture Trip. (2017, September 26). *K-Pop Band BTS Have Made the Best Song About Why It's So Hard to Be a Millennial*. Retrieved from https://theculturetrip.com/asia/south-korea/articles/k-pop-band-bts-have-made-the-best-song-about-why-its-so-hard-to-be-a-millennial/

130. Billboard. (2017, November 29). *BTS's 'Spring Day' Explores the Hardship of Missing Your Loved Ones: See the Translated Lyrics*. Retrieved from https://www.billboard.com/articles/columns/k-town/8053973/bts-spring-day-lyrics-english-translation

131. The New York Times. (2015, April 16). *Snub at Sewol Ferry Memorial Shows Rawness of Wounds in South Korea*. Retrieved from https://www.nytimes.com/2015/04/17/world/asia/park-geun-hye-sewol-ferry-disaster-anniversary-memorial-in-south-korea.html

132. Omonatheydidnt. (2017, February 18). *BTS talks about Billboard 100, Sewol Ferry Tragedy, and "Glass Ceiling."* Retrieved from https://omonatheydidnt.livejournal.com/19762270.html

133. Youtube. (2017, February 21). *BTS Spring Day MV Explained*. Retrieved from https://www.youtube.com/watch?v=Tye1ONFeKis

134. BBC. (2014, May 4). *South Korea ferry survivors 'miscounted.'* Retrieved from https://www.bbc.com/news/world-asia-27314331

135. Genius. *Epilogue: Young Forever*. Retrieved from https://genius.com/Genius-english-translations-bts-epilogue-young-forever-english-translation-lyrics

136. SBS. (2018, January 30). *BTS' RM & Suga open about depression and anxiety*. Retrieved from https://www.sbs.com.au/popasia/blog/2018/01/30/bts-rm-suga-open-about-depression-and-anxiety

137. Reddit. *Exclusive Interview: BTS "Behind our success is sincerity and ability, not social media*. Retrieved from https://www.reddit.com/r/bangtan/comments/7thtn4/180128_exclusive_interview_bts_behind_our_success/dtclyeu/

138. Genius. *Blood, Sweat, and Tears*. Retrieved from https://genius.com/Genius-english-translations-bts-blood-sweat-and-tears-english-translation-lyrics

139. Genius. *Answer: Love Myself*. Retrieved from https://genius.com/Genius-english-translations-bts-answer-love-myself-english-translation-lyrics

Chapter 10

140. The Telegraph. (2019, August 7). *The Korean Beatles: how BTS are changing the language of pop*. Retrieved from https://www.telegraph.co.uk/music/artists/behind-scenes-bts-korean-beatles-defy-boy-band-tradition-demand/

141. Teen Vogue. (2019, June 24). *Criticism of BTS Is Often Just Xenophobia in Disguise*. Retrieved from https://www.teenvogue.com/story/bts-criticism-xenophobia-in-disguise

142. Vulture. (2019, October 2). *The BTS Army Is Ready to Spill Blood Over a New Profile of the Band*. Retrieved from https://www.vulture.com/2019/10/bts-hollywood-reporter-cover-fans-react.html

143. Frederick Joseph Twitter. Retrieved from https://twitter.com/FredTJoseph/status/1190959723698364417

144. The Hollywood Reporter. (2019, October 2). *BTS Is Back: Music's Billion-Dollar Boy Band Takes the Next Step*. Retrieved from https://www.hollywoodreporter.com/features/bts-is-back-musics-billion-dollar-boy-band-takes-next-step-1244580

145. The Atlantic. (2019, July 18). *I wasn't a fan of BTS. And then I was*. Retrieved from https://www.theatlantic.com/entertainment/archive/2019/07/bts-paved-the-way-army-fandom/592543/?fbclid=IwAR3L6pUlba65WYV136fg9orfZPw4SwQWVY8NM9W4msxZruW-wQPycoLB1oSw

146. Huffington Post. (2017, May 23). *Billboard Music Awards 2017: Backlash over BTS Win proves how racist people can be*. Retrieved from https://www.huffingtonpost.ca/2017/05/23/bts-billboard-music-awards-2017_n_16768224.html

147. Buzzfeed News. (2017, May 22). *People are stressing Asian representation after BTS made history at the Billboard Music Awards*. Retrieved from https://www.buzzfeednews.com/article/tanyachen/bts-win-and-asian-representation

148. Australia BTS Twitter. *9 Now broadcast on BTS*. Retrieved from https://twitter.com/australiabts/status/1141320166904496128?lang=en

149. Hypebae. (2019, July 23). *BTS fans are not happy with the 2019 MTV VMAs' new K-Pop Award category*. Retrieved from https://hypebae.com/2019/7/bts-fans-mtv-vmas-video-music-awards-k-pop-category-twitter-backlash

150. Variety. (2019, August 26). *BTS wins first VMA in controversial K-Pop category*. Retrieved from https://variety.com/2019/music/news/bts-vmas-kpop-category-mtv-1203314934/?fbclid=IwAR0WJvewERRjifXmHYAywW2tlYuYaJH4o446bucJK2G2w5H1bM9Eq6dNFIl

151. Metro UK. (2017, November 22). *BTS happy they weren't treated as a 'curious novelty' act at AMAs*. Retrieved from https://metro.co.uk/2017/11/22/bts-happy-they-werent-treated-as-a-curious-novelty-act-at-amas-7100536/

152. The Korea Times. (2019, June 30). *Korea, racism, and BTS*. Retrieved from http://www.koreatimes.co.kr/www/opinion/2019/07/715_271470.html?fbclid=IwAR3grcrmw_lgjUH4v-sONJEUwuFFwPFiQXMI5SEQT_5Xf0OhObIczrWm0WA

153. The Korea Times. (2019, August 4). *BTS vs Dave*. Retrieved from https://m.koreatimes.co.kr/pages/article.asp?newsIdx=273353

154. MTV News. (2020, February 6). *Why do critics love Bong Joon Ho and dismiss BTS*. Retrieved from http://www.mtv.com/news/3155318/bts-bong-joon-ho-critics/

155. The Oscars. (2020, February 10). *Parasite wins 4 Oscars and makes Oscar history*. Retrieved from https://oscar.go.com/news/winners/parasite-wins-4-oscars-and-makes-oscar-history

156. Vivid Seats. *Bangtan Boys Ticket Information*. Retrieved from https://www.vividseats.com/concerts/bangtan-boys-tickets.html#BTSFanStats

157. AllKpop. (2017, July 25). *BTS Fan Demographics*. Retrieved from https://www.allkpop.com/forum/threads/bts-fan-demographics.120139/

158. Teen Vogue. (2020, January 6). *"Parasite" Director Bong Joon Ho Praised BTS on the Golden Globes 2020 Carpet*. Retrieved from https://www.teenvogue.com/story/parasite-director-bong-joon-ho-praised-bts-golden-globes-2020-carpet

Chapter 12

159. Genius. *A Supplementary Story: You Never Walk Alone*. Retrieved from https://genius.com/Genius-english-translations-bts-a-supplementary-story-you-never-walk-alone-english-translation-lyrics

160. Forbes. (2019, July 10). *BTS is the World's highest paid boy band and K-Pop act*. Retrieved from https://www.forbes.com/sites/monicamercuri/2019/07/10/bts-is-the-worlds-highest-paid-boy-band-and-k-pop-act/#6508dd4ae674

161. AllKpop. (2019, June 9). *BTS estimated to have a $4.6 billion impact on Korea's economy annually*. Retrieved from https://www.allkpop.com/article/2019/06/bts-estimated-to-have-a-46-billion-impact-on-koreas-economy-annually

162. Yonhap News Agency. (2018, December 18). *K-pop group BTS's annual economic value estimated at 4 tln won: report*. Retrieved from https://en.yna.co.kr/view/AEN20181218003600320

163. Koreaboo. *The Key Difference Between Korean ARMYs, and International ARMYs*. Retrieved from https://www.koreaboo.com/rewind/key-difference-korean-armys-international-armys/?fbclid=IwAR1NLR6kZE1LtVf7Bmd__MG1gb97KRYcqU2bpLcBls6hazApS2z0TRqlAZQ

164. Spotify Newsroom. (2018, October 11). *K-Pop Takes Over, From 'Gangnam Style' to Global Domination*. Retrieved from https://newsroom.spotify.com/2018-10-11/k-pop-takes-over-from-gangnam-style-to-global-domination/

165. Genius. *Anpanman*. Retrieved from https://genius.com/Genius-english-translations-bts-anpanman-english-translation-lyrics

166. The Korea Times. (2019, July 5). *Billboard columnist says BTS, the Beatles comparable*. Retrieved from https://www.koreatimes.co.kr/www/art/2019/07/732_271802.html

167. Chicago Tribune. (2018, September 6). *Review: In its tour opener, BTS disrupted the whole idea of boy-band masculinity*. Retrieved from https://www.chicagotribune.com/la-et-ms-bts-tour-staples-center-review-20180906-story.html

168. Love Myself. Retrieved from https://www.love-myself.org/eng/home/

169. UNICEF. (2018, September 24). *We have learned to love ourselves, so now I urge you to 'speak yourself.'* Retrieved from https://www.unicef.org/press-releases/we-have-learned-love-ourselves-so-now-i-urge-you-speak-yourself

170. AllKpop. (2019, May 31). *BTS's JIN has become a member of the Korean UNICEF's 'Honours Club.'* Retrieved from https://www.allkpop.com/article/2019/05/btss-jin-has-become-a-member-of-the-korean-unicefs-honours-club

171. South China Morning Post. (2019, March 11). *K-pop 'birthday boy' Suga of BTS donates US$90,000 to sick children's charity as he turns 26*. Retrieved from https://www.scmp.com/magazines/style/people-events/article/2189549/k-pop-birthday-boy-suga-bts-donates-us90000-sick

172. Soompi. (2019, April 6.) *BTS's Jimin Makes Thoughtful Donation For Students In His Hometown Of Busan*. Retrieved from https://www.soompi.com/article/1315425wpp/btss-jimin-makes-thoughtful-donation-for-students-in-his-hometown-of-busan

173. Grammy. (2018, September 19). *BTS On The Creative Process, Breaking Records, Their Responsibility As Artists & More*. Retrieved from https://www.grammy.com/grammys/news/bts-creative-process-breaking-records-their-responsibility-artists-more

174. Genius. *Magic Shop*. Retrieved from https://genius.com/Genius-english-translations-bts-magic-shop-english-translation-lyrics

As for their international activities, it looks like there are some things with BTS that the fans have come to love that will remain the same. Bang maintains that they have no plans to release an all-English album as of yet, saying that the band hopes to stay true to their identity as Korean artists. "I hope the case people have seen with BTS is not just one-time thing and more people to take it as an example. I want many to take that model and get inspiration so that more K-pop singers can make their way to overseas markets. If we teach English to singers and sign a contract with American companies to release albums, then that is no longer part of K-Pop. It is like Asian singers making a debut onto the American market. That is not a sustainable model," Bang told a Korean newspaper.

You gave me the best of me
So you'll give you the best of you
You found me. You knew me
You gave me the best of me
So you'll give you the best of you
— **BTS, "Magic Shop"**[174]

From K-pop idols and Korean tourism ambassadors to youth representatives and motivators, BTS has come a long way. "For us, it will always be important to keep working hard, dancing better, writing better songs, touring, and setting an example. We are living a dream, all seven of us, being able to pursue what we love," RM told *Time*. All of the members often credit the fans as the ones that made it all happen. "I think it's really the fans that gave us the wings that allowed us to fly to where we are now, so we are always thankful," V said.

With growing interest in BTS, it's inevitable that people will always anticipate and want to know what's next for the band. RM, being his philosophical self, can only give an enigmatic answer. "In Korean, the word 'future' is made up of two parts," he told *Billboard*. "The first part means 'not,' and the second means 'to come.' In that sense, 'future' means something that will not come. This is to say: The future is now, and our now is us living our future."